10 Time
Management
Choices

THAT CAN CHANGE
YOUR LIFE

10 Time
Management
Choices

THAT CAN CHANGE
YOUR LIFE

SANDRA FELTON & MARSHA SIMS

Revell

a division of Baker Publishing Group
Grand Rapids, Michigan

© 2009 by Sandra Felton and Marsha Sims

Published by Revell
a division of Baker Publishing Group
PO Box 6287, Grand Rapids, MI 49516-6287
www.revellbooks.com

Repackaged edition published 2021
ISBN 978-0-8007-3955-3

Previously published in 2009 under the title *Organizing Your Day* and in 2015 under the title *Ten Time Management Choices That Can Change Your Life*

Printed in the United States of America

The Library of Congress has cataloged the original edition as follows:
Felton, Sandra.
    Organizing your day : time management techniques that will work for you
/ Sandra Felton and Marsha Sims.
        p. cm.
    Includes bibliographical references.
    ISBN 978-0-8007-3315-5 (pbk.)
    1. Time management. I. Sims, Marsha. II. Title.
HD69.T54F45 2009
650.1'1—dc 22   2008052291

ISBN 978-0-8007-4041-2 (hardcover)

21   22   23   24   25   26   27   7   6   5   4   3   2   1

Each morning sees some task begun,
Each evening sees it close;
Something attempted, something done,
Has earned a night's repose.

Henry Wadsworth Longfellow
"The Village Blacksmith"

contents

Introduction   9

1. Something Strange Has Happened to Time: Too Many Options   15
2. Complications of Time Management: Being Willing to Make the Necessary Changes   24
3. Change for the Better: Adjustments That Work   33
4. If Things Were Perfect: Set Goals for Your Life   45
5. Handling Activity Clutter: Four Dynamic Methods   54
6. Measure Your Time: Keep a Time Log   66
7. Modern Multitasking: Help and Hindrance   74
8. Perfectionism: Helpful or Harmful?   83
9. Procrastination: Overcoming a Nonproductive Tendency   90
10. Easy Project Management: Getting Started   108
11. Working with Your Projects: The Project Notebook   117

12. To-Do List: Keep on Top of Your Important
    Activities 124

13. Delegate: Build a Team 131

14. Interruptions: Regain Control of Your Time 142

15. Time Wasters: Take Charge 153

16. Scheduling Routines: An Indispensable Tool 161

17. Daily Scheduling: Move Smoothly through the
    Day 171

18. Scheduling Tools: Calendars, PDAs, Day
    Planners 177

19. Chronic Lateness: Understanding and Curing the
    Problem 187

20. Creating Powerful Habits: Surefire Methods That
    Work 194

21. Organize Your Space at Home: De-stress Your Life and
    Free Yourself 203

22. Organize Your Business or Home Office: Ensure
    Maximum Productivity 215

23. Organize Your Papers: The Joy of Clear Surfaces and
    Neat Files 225

24. Make the Most of Life: Manage Your
    Opportunities 235

Activities for Ten Time Management Choices 243

Resources 265

introduction

We have discovered something we want to share with you: time management can be fun. Oh, maybe not birthday party fun or Disney World fun or winning-the-game fun. But nothing beats the satisfaction of coming to the end of the day and feeling it was successful. That's real fun!

After we have a good time at Disney World, we come away saying, "Disney did a good job." But when we come to the end of a satisfying day in which we accomplished significant things, we look back and say, "I did a good job." In the long run, that feeling adds a lot more to life than a good vacation.

Sometimes we are admonished to remember that we are human "beings," not human "doings." But people are designed to be doers, to accomplish significant things during our time on earth. What we actually hate is to choke our lives up with low-priority activities that mean nothing at the end of the day. We recoil from wasting our lives on a myriad of things that have little or no significance in the long run.

One of the goals of this book is to help you accomplish easily and quickly those necessary but uninspiring activities that comprise much of our daily lives so you can turn your attention to the significant things you want to do. As you read and use the ideas in this book, you will begin to notice that piles of paper are no longer on your desk at work, and piles of clothes are slowly disappearing at home. The bills are getting paid. You are able to get home in the evening on time because you have eliminated time wasters at work. Somehow, when you manage your time, things that used to be neglected just get done.

Another goal is to help you turn your heart and mind to the excitement of discovering the things that are really important in your life and getting those done. For most people that will mean two things: deepening personal relationships with family and friends and accomplishing meaningful projects.

Some of us have a hard time creating and using systems. Either we don't have the skills to design a system or we design one that is so complicated we can't maintain it. In some cases, once we find a really good system, we have trouble being consistent. This is the reason we have boiled the secrets of successful time management down to the big ten we spotlight at the end of this introduction. Focus on these. Weave several into your life over a period of time and one day you will wake up and find your life has changed.

When you discover the power of managing what goes on in your daily life so that it works better than you ever thought possible, you may want to let out a little shout of joy. As your life becomes vigorous with significant accomplishments, you will feel a surge of enthusiasm.

But first, there are problems to be solved. "The time is out of joint; O cursed spite, that ever I was born to set it right!" was how Shakespeare's Hamlet expressed his personal problem.

What has that to do with us? Hamlet has little to do with us, unless you are reading this book because you also have a problem with time that is out of joint and needs to be set right. Like him, you are the only one who can do what it takes to fix it.

This leads us to the twofold question of this book: Why are you (like many of us) having problems with time management and what can you do to change things for the better? In other words, how can you move from the dark clouds Hamlet was sitting under into the whoohoo! sunlight you are looking for?

When you finish this book, you will know these two things: how your time got out of joint and how to set it right. Once you have acted on what you know, we want to hear the shouting.

●●●

Let us hear from you. After you have read this book and made changes that benefit your life and the lives of those who matter to you, you want someone to know what you have done and to care. We care and would love to hear your good reports.

Contact Sandra at www.messies.com and/or Marsha at www.sortitout.net.

True or false?

1. Life seems to be getting more frenetic.
2. I want my life to count for more.
3. I am looking for a time management system that really works.

If you answered true to any of these you will enjoy this book. Read on!

10 time management choices that can change your life

The following are choices you can make to bring needed change to your life. The chapters indicated will fill you in on what you need to know, so you can fold them into your life one at a time. When you have successfully added one, go on to another.

1. Dream Big—Chapter 4

Dare to wonder what your life would be like if your time worked out just right, if it were (gasp!) perfect. Don't skip over this as a superfluous exercise. Remember the old saying: He who aims at nothing is likely to hit it. The opposite is also true: He who aims carefully at something is likely to hit it.

2. Focus: Keep the Main Thing the Main Thing—Chapter 5

Creative and interesting people have many areas about which they are enthusiastic. They overextend themselves in their passion for life. Keep the passion but learn how to prioritize so you will accomplish the goals that are most important to you.

3. Do It Now—Chapter 9

There are two kinds of procrastination that plague us all: procrastination of the urgent and less critical but chronic procrastination. No matter what kind is holding you back from doing what needs to be done when it needs to be done, you can get yourself unstuck.

4. Take Control of Your Projects—Chapters 10, 11, 12

Some projects are simple and it is easy to let the ball drop on these. Some projects are complicated and we need a method to clarify the steps. You will be surprised at how your life will move forward as you apply the principles found in these chapters to all of your projects.

5. Delegate, Delegate, Delegate—Chapter 13

Should you delegate a responsibility? To whom? How do you go about it? Delegating well so you can use your time efficiently is an important part of a life well lived. The key? Just do it!

6. Manage Interruptions, Distractions, and Time Wasters—Chapters 14, 15

None of us lives on a desert island. In this era of electronic communication, we are more likely to be interrupted than ever before. In addition, internal distractions creep in to dissipate our time.

7. Make and Use an Effective Schedule—Chapters 16, 17

A well-crafted schedule is a wonderful thing. It's like a powerful engine in a car and will move your life forward.

8. Use the Right Tools—Chapter 18

To have the greatest success in sticking to a schedule, you need the right tools. Whether you develop them yourself or buy what is on the market, the right tools will be invaluable. Some people don't want to be bothered with tools. Bad idea. Check out what is available and choose what meets your need and your personality.

9. Hang On to a Few Powerful Habits—Chapter 20

People who manage their time well have developed a few consistently applied and useful habits. Weaving some of what you learn in this chapter into your life will free you from unnecessary time wasters.

10. Organize Your Space—Chapters 21, 22, 23

"Stuff" in the way, "stuff" to be cared for—these impede our progress and demand our time. Whether papers are piling up in your office or out-of-place items are messing up your home, decluttering your life will free you to do what is really important.

No matter what is holding you back, you can overcome it. Choose to incorporate these ten habits into your life. Your productivity will soar as will your personal satisfaction. There is a wonderfully upgraded life waiting for you. Just begin one step at a time to move in that direction.

1 something strange has happened to time

too many options

Yesterday is a canceled check; tomorrow is a promissory note; today is the only cash you have. Spend it wisely.

Anonymous

If you think people in today's world have a unique problem with time, you are absolutely correct. While we were not paying attention, something happened. That something is progress. Modern advancement is like a wonderful train full of good things for our lives. It transports prosperity and convenience beyond the dreams of the past, and even beyond the reach of many in today's world, but it brings some baggage as well.

In his book *Margin*, Richard A. Swenson uses an enlightening illustration. Let us suppose that a five-hundred-car train were bound for a needy third world village, loaded with medicine, automobiles, libraries, food, recreational equipment, and a good supply of gold.

Scattered randomly among the five hundred cars, however, were fifty cars containing deadly viruses, pollutants, poisonous gases, illicit drugs, and nuclear weapons poised to explode if they were jostled.

That's the way it is with modern progress. Some very good things have come our way, but unexpected problems have gotten into the mix—among them our problem with time.

Time got very much out of joint when technology entered modern life. The average American spends thirty-one and a half hours a week watching television (2006, Nielson). Yikes! That's almost a second job. We spend more time commuting, since the automobile has made it possible to travel farther to work. The cell phone connects us to more and more people wherever we are, so we can talk many more hours. When modern household conveniences made cooking, cleaning, and laundry easier, women raised their standard of housekeeping and added other time-consuming pursuits as well. Life got less physical but more hectic.

In short, modern conveniences give us more options, more opportunities, and increased stimulation to participate in more activities. That's good. But many activities are time wasters. That's bad. It is such a good train, many of us have not realized that it has muddled up our lives in ways our grandpa did not have to worry about. People are feeling the pressure. As a result, an important concept is growing more and more important in modern life—time management, which is really activity management, which actually boils down to self-management.

Our job in this book is to identify and derail the time management difficulties that got mixed in with the good life we have developed for ourselves. This book spotlights realistically the issues you and many people just like you face every day. As you read about people in real situations facing actual problems, you will begin to recognize the strategies you can apply to bring you real success both at home and on the job.

As you read this book, spot your personal problems with time management so you can set about getting rid of them.

The Problems Look Something like This

You come into work early and leave late and tired. You want a change. In short, you are overwhelmed.

Or you work all day at home, and when your husband comes in, looks around, and asks what you've been doing all day, you have trouble knowing what to say, because you aren't really sure.

What is the problem, or better yet, what is the solution?

Michael

Michael's company downsized and let his co-worker go. Now Michael's doing two jobs in middle management and calling it one. Stress is building. He has just found out he has high blood pressure. He needs help and he needs it quickly.

No matter how diligently he focuses, he's not able to get his work done, even though he's efficient, on top of things, and hardworking. In addition to his regular tasks, his bosses schedule meetings over which he has no control. Often he is interrupted by people calling or dropping in unannounced. Unfortunately, he is not good at delegating and his assistant isn't very helpful anyway.

At the end of one particularly rough week, he had hardly any energy left for his wife and children. He thought, I *need help*. I *don't want to keep going like this*.

Many of today's employees have to work harder and longer to get their work done, especially since downsizing means they have to carry a heavier load. A third of those in middle management are frustrated with their life-work balance according to USA *Today*. Michael was one of that group.

Linda

Linda teaches fourth grade. She is going to have a larger class this year so she will have extra paperwork. She is an excellent teacher but somehow never learned how to do the paperwork efficiently. She does report cards at the last minute and other reports are often tardy.

She's a single mom with one son and she cares for her elderly mom. To fit in all of her activities, she stays up late at night and often is late to school.

Each morning Linda has to exercise, shower, fix breakfast for her son and mom, give her mom her meds, gather her papers, and get in the car by 8:15. At school she wrestles with keeping straight the forms from the office, homework papers, and various kinds of permission slips from the students. During the workday, she has a couple of breaks and she enjoys socializing with her friends in the teachers' lounge. She realizes she could be correcting papers or doing lesson plans but she tells herself she will catch up on work at home.

After school her real job begins. She ferries her son to his activities, helps her mom bathe, washes clothes, cooks, unloads and loads the dishwasher, grades some papers, feeds the dog, handles the mail, answers her emails, and falls into bed exhausted.

As teaching loads become more stressful and increased requirements are added, Linda is feeling the pressure. And the complexities of family life add to the stress. Workers who are part of the sandwich generation, caring for both their parents and their children, like Linda, have an added time crunch at home.

Bernice

Bernice is a happy, self-employed personal coach who works from home. Keeping up with information for her clients, she amasses a great deal of paper on a variety of topics. Her schedule is tight with back-to-back fifty-minute phone appointments. She allows ten minutes between calls and often uses that time to make other calls, prepare for the next client, go to the bathroom, or walk her dog. She seldom takes the time to put the accumulating papers away. As a result, they pile up.

Bernice doesn't have much time to develop friends or read for pleasure. She watches TV primarily for the news as it relates to her clients.

One day follows another. Her work has become her life but it is unsatisfying in some nebulous way she is just beginning to feel. Her spirit is dry. She encourages others to live a balanced life but doesn't take her own advice.

If asked to pinpoint her biggest problem area, she would say it is paper accumulation. However, to the objective observer, it is obvious the problem is one of life balance. Though she coaches others on time management, she does not recognize that she has a problem with it herself.

Bernice is an excellent coach partly because she goes beyond the call of duty for her clients, researching, referring, emailing them forms they can use, and doing anything necessary to make sure they are helped. But she neglects her own needs.

Time management is a vital issue for entrepreneurs like Bernice. They are often creative types whose strengths lie in their freewheeling style not in their organizational skills. But to move their ideas forward, they must harness their creativity with down-to-earth management of their time and activities. Because they are flooded with ideas and see many opportunities to overwork, it is crucial that they use their time productively.

Marshall

Before his date to retire, Marshall counted the days. He had been contemplating it for months. He planned to go to the library and read for hours; he wanted to plant a vegetable garden. He would spend time with friends, teach his grandchildren woodworking skills, learn a foreign language, and volunteer at his church. As he put it, he wanted to sing his song.

But having retired, things were not working out well. One of his projects was to write a book about his life, an important legacy he wanted to leave his family, but he never got far because his daughters would call, a repairman would arrive, or he had to get the oil in his car changed.

Where does all the time go? he wonders after trying his new lifestyle for seven months. Then he says what he has heard many other retirees say, "How did I ever have time to go to work?"

The worst part is he feels incompetent. He remembers when he used to be productive in the workforce and the satisfaction it gave him. If he keeps frittering away his days, he is afraid he will be too old to do all of the things he wants to do and he will leave his song unsung.

Retirement forces people to abandon the idea that it is the job that has been holding them back. For most people the depressing truth is that they have never learned to be organized, disciplined, or motivated on their own. On their jobs they were not solely responsible to be self-starters or self-motivators. Nor did they have to set up their own schedules. The job, with all of its preset requirements, did that for them. A day on the job is more easily organized than a day at home.

Marshall had envisioned his retirement filled with activities that were both enjoyable and significant. Instead, he found himself picking up cleaning, unstopping the toilet, reading the newspaper, watching afternoon TV, and buying groceries. The weeds of everyday living were choking out the activities he had dreamed of doing. As he faced the end of his journey, he was beginning to wake up to the fact that he needed to learn and apply time management skills to his life if he was going to sing that song.

Time Management

We need to emphasize two basic facts before we continue:

1. The focus of time management is priorities and stems from self-management. Self-management is the power-house of time management. Self-management makes it happen. In reality you can't manage elusive time but you can manage the very-much-in-the-now you.
2. Techniques, tricks, systems or whatever you want to call real time management know-how can be very valuable. Some books downplay organizing systems and indicate that if you have enough focus and self-control, you'll be okay. Not so. You need good skills as well.

To make time work for you, you need systems. Without a system, things fall apart. You may have several systems and life is going along swell until you hit a spot for which you have no system. When that happens, you need to develop a new one.

Is Your Time Train on Track?

If you see yourself in any of the four stories above, you are not alone. But it does not have to be this way. Instead of life being a day-to-day drudgery, your life can become a source of pleasure and productivity.

Michael, Linda, Bernice, and Marshall have to recognize the problem before they can find the solutions. All of us who experience these problems must face the same issue—realizing that something needs to change and caring enough to do something about it.

Your Turn

☐ Briefly tell the story of where you are in the area of time management. Which of the stories above sounds the most like you?

☐ Look at the following list and check the areas where your time is out of joint. Add others if you wish.

- family life
- other relationships
- career
- education
- house
- health

☐ What do you already do well? Laundry, dishes, filing, for example.

☐ In what areas do you need to do better? Bill handling, getting out of the house on time every day, for example.

Tips

1. Control your time. Don't let time control you.
2. Be realistic about how long a task will take by timing what you do and writing it down for next time.
3. Locate specifically where you are running into trouble timewise and concentrate on fixing those places.
4. Focus on solutions not problems.
5. Group your activities and you will save time.

Yes or no?

1. Are you trying to do too much in the time you have?
2. Do you know what the chief time hindrances are in your life?
3. Are you willing to make some changes in how you use your time?

If you answered yes to any of these, you are ready for the next chapter.

2 complications of time management

being willing to make the necessary changes

Your power to choose the direction of your life allows you to reinvent yourself, to change your future, and to powerfully influence the rest of creation.

Stephen R. Covey

Time is unpredictable. Often it seems slippery, sliding by unnoticed and unused. Because you can't see it, it is tricky to organize. Let's demystify it. If we approach it in the same way we approach organizing furniture or clothing or silverware, it becomes less mysterious.

Compare time to a bookcase. Any bookcase is limited, by its width and number of shelves, in how many books it can hold. When the space is filled with books both big and small, no more will fit. To put new books on the shelf, old ones must be discarded.

Like the bookshelf, time is finite and can hold only a certain number of activities. If your time is full, and most of us feel ours is, you need to discard activities to make room for the new ones.

People put books in their bookcases in different ways. If you go to one friend's house, you may notice a well-organized, uncrowded bookcase. Books are not squeezed in so tightly they are difficult to pull off the shelf. Often there is extra room at the end of a shelf. The books are grouped according to subject. All stand vertically in a row. The bookshelf looks good and works well.

But you may have another friend who is not so tidy. His (or her) messy bookcase tries to hold more books than it can contain comfortably. Books press tightly against each other and some lie across the tops of others because they don't have room to stand on the shelf. There are no empty areas and they aren't grouped according to subject. Sometimes, in an effort to store more books, your friend will add an additional row of books behind the one that faces out and can be seen. Although this friend's bookshelf holds more books, they are very difficult to locate and use. This is an instance when more really is less.

> Not everything you face can be changed, but everything you change must first be faced.

People use time in ways that are similar to these bookcases. Some, like your neat friend, schedule only what they have time for and organize their activities to fit the available time. They are wise enough to leave some extra time unscheduled to act as a cushion.

Others have the time equivalent of the messy bookshelf. They schedule many activities and don't organize them to fit into the time available. Life is a jumble and many good activities remain undone because the disorganized people can't get to them or forget about them. That's a shame, because many people whose time bookcase is not working are among the most creative and intelligent people around.

But never fear if you are one whose time is crowded and disorganized. We said earlier that time is slippery. It slips in different places for different people. In this chapter we will look at some of those oily places that may trip you up. Then in the next chapter we will look at the choices you can make that will change your life. Slowly but surely we will unpack the information in each of those choices that will enable you to apply their power to your life.

Personal Hindrances

All of us are individuals with different characteristics relating to our use of time. Some people are:

- *Not naturally organized*. There are some of us who are smart but nonetheless have trouble in our careers or other areas of life because we don't naturally plan well, organize time and space, initiate projects, see them through to completion, or stick to long-range goals. Everybody has occasional trouble in these areas, but some of us struggle regularly to do things of an organizational nature. Setting priorities, making decisions, and sequencing are often the most difficult.

- *Distractible*. Some of us are more distractible than others. We find it hard to stick to one thing. At the end of the day we look back at a lot of half-completed projects because, in each case, something drew our attention away from them.

  As a child, Wanda had trouble focusing in school. It wasn't until she became an adult that she discovered she had attention-deficit disorder. *Ah*, she thought, *that's the reason I struggle with trying to keep on track*. Just knowing gave some relief and pointed her in the direction for getting help.

- *Depressed*. People who are discouraged or depressed, perhaps about their poor time management and organizational skills, find it hard to get up the enthusiasm to overcome the problem. Depression is a serious impediment to organizing.

- *Slow moving.* Some people are naturally fast; others are not. Watch the checkers in the grocery store for confirmation of that. If you are a slow mover, you need to be sure you keep going slowly and surely in the right direction. Like the tortoise (of tortoise and hare fame), you will get there eventually; the key is to stay on track.

- *Not healthy.* Some people who are accused of being lazy are not. They are living with low-grade infections, like mono; low hormone levels, like thyroid; anemia; subclinical depression; or other problems that need medical attention. Because their condition is not critical, it is often overlooked. Get yourself checked out if you are dragging through life.

- *Just not knowledgeable.* You can't work well in the home if you don't know how to cook or clean efficiently. And you can't do a good job at work if you aren't well trained in your job requirements. Time management is the same. Many time management skills must be learned.

- *Caretakers.* Sometimes, in our desire to be needed, we take on more than we can do because we want to feel important in people's lives. We adopt the "helper" mentality. Typically we don't like to delegate jobs to others. Often, because we do so much ourselves, we fail to train our children or co-workers up to their potential.

- *Overwhelmed.* This is the word that springs most quickly to the lips of those who have way too much to do. If you feel like you are drowning and life is being squeezed of its enjoyment, you probably are saying that you are "overwhelmed."

- *Very creative.* Creative people have trouble setting boundaries on their enthusiasm for ideas or projects. If they have a bookcase, they keep piling more and more onto the shelves. Routine bores creative people. They like to do new things or try things in a new way. Even so, routine is a powerful tool in time management and must be addressed in some way, even by creative people.

Another kind of personal hindrance has to do with your home and/or job site. These places may hold you back in the area of time management. The problem may be:

- *Disorganized space.* If your office or house is a mess, you will lose things or have trouble getting to them even when you know where they are. This applies especially to finding papers in your business. In the home, a much more complex place than the office, the family wastes time looking for keys, shoes, clean clothes, missing bills, the hamster, and other items. Messiness is a huge time waster. Clearing clutter saves time in the future.

- *Poor planning skills.* Some people have never learned time management techniques. Especially when it relates to home activities, the whole idea of time management is an unfamiliar concept. At the job, unless you make the effort to plan your activities, your work will drift into unproductive waters.

- *Not well equipped.* If the computer goes down or the printer does not work, your job comes to a jolting halt. If you have to go down the hall each time you need a stapler or hole punch, you are wasting time. If you chop with a knife when a food chopper would do it in seconds or if you mix by hand instead of with a mixer, you are wasting time. A slow cooker set up in the morning will save a lot of work in the evening. Well-chosen equipment saves time.

- *Others.* Charles can tell you about this problem. His office mate is messy, noisy, and inconsiderate. His boss schedules meetings that keep Charles from his work. His job description is poorly planned and he is saddled with more administrative busywork than necessary. At home his wife and kids disrupt his plans and make more work for him, and he feels they are not carrying their share of the load. Charles is able to manage his time, but others in his life make it impossible for him to stick to his schedule. We must address the problems that other people in our world create.

Playing the Victim

No matter the reason(s) you struggle with time management, you can make a turnaround by doing one thing consistently: make different decisions. When you change behavior, your time management problem will perish like Sennacherib's army that "melted like snow in the glance of the Lord" (Lord Byron, "The Destruction of Sennacherib").

> The difference between "I can't" and "I can" is often "I will."

However, changing behavior is difficult and, if we are not careful, we will drift into old patterns of thinking rather than forge new and uncomfortable territory. Some of those old patterns may include:

- *Blaming.* Darryl is a blamer. He thinks things can't change because the problem is someone else's fault. At work he thinks it is his boss, his co-workers, his assistant, his job description, his work space, or whatever else he can think of that is out of his control. He doesn't try to make changes because it might be too hard or cause trouble.

  At home he blames the family. They are messy and they won't carry their share of the work. Sometimes he thinks his problems are his parents' fault for not teaching him to manage time. Or possibly it is God's fault for not equipping him with an organizing gene.

- *Complaining.* If you complain about your time problems, you exude an aura of competence. By talking about them, you are telegraphing that you see the problems and the assumption is you are going to do something about them. Often complaining substitutes for action.

  Woe to those who live around a complainer who does nothing about his or her problems. The complaints will never stop because the problems will continue. If you are a complainer, stop. If you live or work around a complainer, stay as far away as possible because the negativity of complaints will affect you.

- *Justifying.* "I don't want to be hung up on time management," some say. "People are more important than being a slave to a schedule." A few might say, "That's not my style." Others go so far as to proclaim proudly, "I live loosely so I can be open to whatever comes my way." Still others say, " I rely on the Spirit of God to guide me moment by moment."

  Show me people who justify their behavior by being philosophically opposed to time management, and I will show you people who are wasting a good part of their life. God gave them time to use wisely. They are unlike the servant in the parable of the talents who invested his money wisely and got more for his boss. They are more like the guy who just sat on his money (buried it) and was punished by the boss for poor management.

Solutions

Step away from blaming, complaining, and justifying. No matter what is holding you back, you can overcome it. There is a wonderfully upgraded life waiting for you. The ten choices you read at the end of the introduction contain the answers to all of these issues. Just begin one step at a time to move in the direction of good time management.

Open yourself to possibilities you might not have considered before. In the next chapter we will talk about significant changes you can make to take control of your time and life

Your Turn

☐ Which of the hindrances in this chapter resonated the most with you? Put your finger on the ones that seem to fit your situation. Check as many as are relevant to you.

___ not naturally organized

___ distractible

___ depressed

___ move slowly

___ not healthy

___ not knowledgeable

___ a caretaker

___ overwhelmed

___ very creative

___ live and work in messy spaces

___ poor planning skills

___ not well equipped

___ others disrupt plans

___ blaming

___ complaining

___ justifying

☐ Next to the ones you've checked, write down the first thing you can do to correct the problem.

Tips

1. Plan ahead how you will use the twenty-four hours in your day.
2. Tackle hard things early so they won't be hanging over your head.
3. Plan to use your peak productivity time to your best advantage.
4. Think and plan first. Act second.
5. Do things now that will save you time in the future.

Yes or no?

1. Do you want to say no but often feel that you can't?
2. Are you a very responsible person and often carry more than your share of the load?
3. Are you ready to evaluate what changes you can make?

If you answered yes to any of these questions, you will benefit from the next chapter.

---

3 change for the better

adjustments that work

No problem can stand the assault of sustained thinking.

Voltaire

Time marches forward without thought. It cannot be controlled. If we think about it, we realize that what we call "time management" really means "self-management in relation to how we use our time." The good news is you have full control of your time management problems. The control lies within yourself. The bad news is that, to make an improvement in your time management, you must take charge of yourself. This is not really bad news but it will seem like it initially. Once you come to terms with the concept, you will find that self-control is one of the most enjoyable and empowering characteristics any of us can develop.

The issue of time management is never about the stuff, the boss, the environment, the size of your space, the co-workers, or the amount of email you get. It is about governing yourself so you can control your environment.

Managing time is about what you are thinking or not thinking, doing or not doing. Your thoughts and actions determine your ability to control your time, which is the essence of your life.

Changing your life for the better involves that frightening word *change*. Not all bad words have four letters. Some have six, like this key word in self-management, C-H-A-N-G-E. Even when it is for the better and we want to do it, it is hard to alter our lives.

Iris found that out by experience.

Friendly Iris Manages Her Margins

I really cannot give you the formula for success. But I can give you the formula for failure. It's this: Try to please everyone.

Bernard Meltzer

Iris worked the front desk in a downtown office. She was the ambassador of first impressions for her company. Her job was to greet and care for the needs of visitors and to answer the phone pleasantly. She did her job with pride. Since she was friendly and helpful by nature, her co-workers started asking her for little favors.

"Iris, will you make a copy of this and stick it in the Jones file on my desk?"

"Iris, can you collate these papers for me?"

Her bubbly attitude was part of her personal life. Her friends and family asked her for little favors too, which she consistently did. She was happy she could help them out.

She built quite a reputation as somebody you could go to for a hand. Slowly as the volume of "little favors" built up, so did Iris's annoyance. Even though she kept saying yes, she did so more and more reluctantly. She was doing so much for others, her own work and her serenity were suffering.

Once Iris realized that she was losing control of her time and life by not protecting reasonable boundaries, she looked for and found effective ways to control her time.

Her written goal was: "By the end of the month, I want to stop having my time abused by my co-workers." She decided to quantify her progress by making a list of the things she was asked to do that were out of her job description and how she managed them. She kept a running tally. By the end of the month she noticed co-workers had begun to slack off asking her for her help as they sensed that Iris's well of helpfulness was running dry.

Lack of preparation on your part does not constitute an emergency on my part.

She maintained margins in her life so she would have enough "white space" to do what she needed to do comfortably. She applied some of the tried-and-true approaches below to slow the flow of favors.

When others ask you for some little favor, be careful not to violate your boundaries by agreeing. Keep in mind that when you say no to something unimportant, it leaves time for saying yes to an important request. Here are some appropriate responses that are kind but definite.

1. Soften your no with a quick, "I'd really like to but I'm afraid I can't." Don't give a reason that could be countered. People who are the most effective at saying no don't give excuses.
2. Offer an alternative or suggest a substitute: "I can't do the filing for you but I can ask someone else to help you."
3. Say yes to part of what they want, like a mom responding to her kids: "We don't have time to go out to eat tonight but we can get a sundae at the drive-through."

4. Use your agreement as a bartering tool: "Sure, I'll help you file these papers if you will type some names into the database before Monday."
5. Couch it as a favor: "I'll be glad to do you a favor." That way you let the person know he or she is indebted timewise to you. Make sure you call in the favor.
6. Help the person find assistance. Say, "I'm not the person to help you with that but I know who can and I can help you locate him."
7. Break the instant-yes habit by stalling, not so much for the other person's sake as for yours, to give you time to work up the courage to say no: "Let me check my schedule before I give you an answer."
8. Reflect a thoughtful evaluation of their request: "I don't think that would be the best use of my time."

Brandon Remains Responsible

Brandon was as unlike Iris as he could be. He was a nose-to-the-grindstone responsible type. A teacher in a private school, Brandon kept a tight rein on his classes and moved his students forward at a rapid pace. This generated a lot of papers to grade, but Brandon was up to the challenge. To solve the problem, he devised a notebook checking system and computerized his grade book so he could enter and calculate his grades quickly.

But all of his efforts to streamline still left him overburdened with work. He proposed an alternative to his principal. In exchange for one less class, he would help with a few administrative tasks. His principal agreed. Before long, however, because Brandon was so dependable, the principal began asking for more and more administrative assistance.

Brandon began to feel used. When he thought about it, he did not blame the principal. He realized he had asked for it by making himself overly available. Brandon had not realized his own limitations. Because being useful was important to him, he spread himself too thin. He was putting himself in the position of those who burn out because they choose to overdo.

Only when he became aware of his situation and kept a log of what he was doing did Brandon start to put the skids on his over-the-top efforts. He wrote his assigned areas of responsibility down and posted them where he could see them. By word and action, he managed to concentrate on doing what he did well. He was still responsible, but in a reasonable way.

Rob Flexes for Success

Rob works for the local power plant. He blamed his time pressures on the fact that his new office was too small. He had moved from a more spacious office to a cubicle when the plant office reorganized according to the suggestions of a business consultant. Rob concluded the consultant knew nothing about the needs of the office staff but he was stuck with the change.

Rob had used a large time line, which required a great deal of wall space. Now it wouldn't fit on his wall. His hit-list goals were also written on paper that was too large to post in his new environment. His three priority goals had been on cards hung right above his desk. These were things he considered invaluable to his productivity and now their usefulness was threatened because he couldn't post them in his small space.

In addition, his cubicle was noisy. Other phone conversations distracted him. And his smaller desk was littered with awards, gifts from clients, family pictures, a myriad of pens, and a pitiful little plant.

What irked him the most was the doughnut lady who came by with her cart each morning and afternoon and parked right outside his doorway. People stopped working and gathered around the cart for socializing. Sometimes, since the cart was outside his door, in addition to the chatter, people would drop in to ask for change or to visit. Rob's productivity plummeted. He blamed everything around him for his dilemma.

What part of no do you not understand, the N or the O?

Something had to change. Rob's desperation drove him to action. He reworked his time line to fit on legal-sized paper that could easily go on his cubicle wall. He put his hit-list goals on five-by-eight-inch index cards and hung them under his time chart. He put a shortcut for easy access to the time line and his hit list on his laptop. Now he was back in business. Being willing to make these changes was a turning point for Rob. He moved on to make other alterations in the way he did things.

He discovered that the conference room was empty in the morning. When he heard the doughnut lady coming, he used it as a signal to grab a cup of coffee and his computer and move to the quiet of the conference room to make calls and schedule appointments. He began to look forward to the quiet midmorning break.

He made other adjustments as well. With some resentment, he boxed the personal items that had been on his larger desk. Soon he discovered, to his surprise, that he really enjoyed his clear work space.

It turned out that the changes were a mixed bag. Some things were worse since the move but some things were definitely better. Everything could be handled. His productivity rose to its previous level, and he realized that all that time he had spent grousing and stewing had been counterproductive.

Learning What Works

Iris, Brandon, and Rob learned how to make changes so they could make the best use of their time. Here are several pointers that can work for each of us.

Be Realistic

Healthy optimism is a wonderful thing when it is part of an overall package of vigorous, positive behavior. Like "the little engine that could," when you think you can ("I think I can! I think I can!"), you draw on deeper reserves to huff and puff to the top of the hill.

However, there is a kind of unproductive optimism that undermines determination. This is seen in the person who hopes for the best and says to herself, *Why bother with the discipline of time management? Things usually work out pretty well anyway.* This kind of thinking encourages lazy work habits and casual living instead of striving for excellence and dedicating oneself to important objectives.

It's important to have goals, but it's also essential to be realistic about what it will take to achieve your goals.

Be Focused

Sports are full of slogans designed to focus the team, like, "Winning is not the main thing. Winning is the only thing." Sports have the advantage that they are played in a restricted area during a limited length of time. But the game of life is more complicated. It has fewer parameters and more activities, so it's easy to wander from focusing on our big priorities and begin pursuing less important activities. Besides, we don't have a coach reminding us constantly to stay focused.

In everyday life, focus is fueled by enthusiasm. If you have a wonderful goal you are dreaming about, you are much more likely to stick with it till you reach it. Don Aslett, the Cleaning

Guru, puts it this way in his book *How to Handle 1,000 Things at Once*, "Knowing and seriously pursuing what you want is the real source of personal management."

Be Hopeful

You *can* make your life better. Through time management your life can be more productive and enjoyable. It does not have to be pressured and out of control. Before you can move forward, however, you must be convinced there is a reason for trying and that if you try, you can succeed.

Be Proactive

Nip problems in the bud before they become bigger. Stop junk mail, unwanted phone solicitations, email spam, and other modern intrusions on your life. Check the information on the direct marketing website: http://www.dmachoice.org/consumerassistance.html.

Make a schedule to guide your regular daily activities. Print it out and post it. Or put it on your desktop calendar, to-do list, or planner. Use either a kitchen timer or your computer schedule reminder to ding when it is time to change activities.

Make permanent lists for things you do over and over. This could be a packing list that you put in your suitcase so you don't have to rethink your packing needs each trip you take. Or a list of all the things you normally buy at the grocery store, in the order of your path through your favorite store. Keep lists on documents in your computer for updating or printing out when needed. (More about schedules and lists in future chapters.)

Be Self-Aware

Each one of us is different and requires a different approach to time management. If you are a morning person, it makes sense to schedule high-priority tasks early in the day. In the afternoon do drudge activities, like filing or folding laundry. If you need quiet to concentrate, go into work before the gang arrives or schedule bill paying while the kids are at school.

Be Persistent

Learning any new and complex activity takes patience. If one thing does not fit, try another and another until you find what works for you. In this book, several methods are given for you to try. Don't give up until you have found what makes your life more productive and enjoyable. You may have to start new habits like friendly Iris or disappear into another area like successful Rob. With persistence, most problems can be lessened and sometimes even solved.

Be Alert

To make progress, we need to be very aware of what is happening around us. It may be that we need to notice our physical space. Often people look behind them at the end of the day and are surprised to see the debris they have left there. They were unaware of what was happening. It takes concentration, practice, and desire to break the habit of working in a distracted way.

Organized people are keenly aware of surfaces that are clear and they make it a point to keep them that way. This involves returning items to the place where they belong—bottles back to the refrigerator, clothes hung up in the closet, and the like, because organized people are keenly aware of how distracting clutter can be. In the Messies Anonymous organization, this habit is known as "Stow as you go!" Discarding trash as it is encountered is known as "Throw as you go!" Keep these directives in your mind and say them aloud to yourself and to others during the day. Hang them as posters and put them on your screensaver. Your time will magically increase if you follow these battle cries.

At the office, organized people keep the desk, credenza, and chairs free of papers because they are alert to how much time it takes to go back and clear up what is left out.

People who are alert to time management can see the problems arising from being interrupted, avoiding scheduling, using space poorly, and other interferences with their time use. Once they spot trends, they begin to address the problems.

Unless you are alert to your surroundings and activities, your use of time will spiral into chaos and you will not know what caused it. Maintain alertness, and if that does not come naturally for you, bring in someone who seems to be perceptive to help you spot things that are interfering with your efficiency.

The Process of Change

As you read through this book and consider your life, your thinking about your use of time will be transformed. Like Iris, Brandon, and Rob, you will have opportunities to choose to make a few significant changes that will help you reach your goals, and you will realize:

If I change my thinking, I will change my feelings.
If I change my feelings, I will change my actions.
If I change my actions, I will change my life.

Significant transformation must be finessed into life by moving changes slowly but surely into place. As we have already suggested, begin to apply the ten principles already given. After one principle becomes a part of your life, choose another and keep moving down the list. As you do so, the quality of your life will take a giant leap forward.

Now hold your breath and take the biggest step of all, as presented in the next chapter—dare to dream big.

Your Turn

☐ We made many suggestions in this chapter for improving the control of your life. Which one(s) do you need to adopt?

___ Be realistic.

___ Be focused.

___ Be hopeful.

___ Be proactive.

___ Be self-aware.

___ Be persistent.

___ Be alert.

☐ This week, handle your responsibilities right away. Make a list of what needs to be done and cross off items as they are completed.

☐ Make reminders of "Stow as you go!" and "Throw as you go!" and place them in prominent places.

Tips

1. Always have a goal clarifying what you want to accomplish.
2. Plan your work, then work your plan.
3. Make small, gradual improvements daily.
4. Welcome changes, whether you think of them or they are suggested by others.

5. Focus on important habit changes.
6. Look for the positives in every situation.

Yes or no?

1. Have you taken the time to evaluate what you really want out of life?
2. Do you know the best way to capture your dreams?
3. Do you have a sense of purpose for your life?

If you answered no to one or more of these questions, you will benefit from the next chapter.

---

4 if things were perfect

set goals for your life

> The number one reason most people don't get what they want is that they don't know what they want.
>
> T. Harv Eker
> *Secrets of the Millionaire Mind*

At some point each of us must step back and look at what our lives have become and think about what we wish we had done. This is what Michael, Linda, Bernice, and Marshall, whom we met earlier, did, each in his or her own way. As they did so, they began to change the direction of their lives.

Making Changes

If you recall, when we left Michael, frustration had driven him to step back and look at the life he was living and to dream of what could be if he could ever get it under control. He was wishing that he wouldn't have multiple uncompleted assignments and his boss would be more realistic about how much one person can handle. If life were perfect, he would have an assistant who would take more responsibility without needing careful supervision. He wouldn't have so many interruptions. He would regain a sense of satisfaction with his work and arrive home with enough enthusiasm and energy to enjoy his family and participate in the things he feels are important—church activities, fly fishing, playing in the yard with the kids, taking his wife out, and some important home improvement projects he'd been putting off.

> We create our tomorrow by what we dream today.

And what about Linda of the sandwich generation? Clearly Linda needed a break. She had way too much on her shoulders and no relief was in sight. She had time to think only when she was driving to school.

Today, as Linda was daydreaming about a peaceful life, she decided to do something a little different and focus on specific categories of her life. She asked herself how her life would be different if everything were perfect.

- She would have time to play with her son and have fun with him—at least thirty minutes a day.
- She would spend more time with her mom, soaking up her wisdom and her support.
- She would have time to read for pleasure, as she used to, and go shopping for frivolous things, even if she didn't buy.
- She would talk about social things with her friends and not think about work.
- Her school paperwork would be under control and up-to-date.

Bernice was also doing some thinking. She decided to take a vacation from her personal coaching, her first break in five years. She and her sister booked a cruise. As they sailed, they talked about what they were doing and how it was working for them. After taking time to look at her overwhelmed lifestyle, Bernice applied some of her own advice and started to make a list of the specific areas she wanted to improve.

The problem of paper piles, magazines, too much to read, and unanswered mail was at the top of her list. Other concerns were no time to spend with her dog, whom she loved, feeling rushed and harried, and not having enough time to relax. She felt she was suffering the pain of success. At first, her full plate made her proud but now it was wearing her down. Her success had become her albatross. She was starting to wonder if work was all there was in life.

She had always thought that the papers were her chief problem, but when she thought about it, she realized her real problem was that she did not manage her time well. Actually she wanted a better quality of life and time to do the things that were really meaningful to her. Even if the papers disappeared, she would still have a time problem.

> When you start daydreaming in detail, it becomes planning.

Having listed her problems, Bernice began to describe her dream of how she really wanted things to be in each area, how things would be if they were perfect.

- Instead of piles of paper everywhere, there would be clear surfaces, no paper anywhere.
- Instead of too much mail, she would receive less mail each day.
- Instead of unread magazines, she would store the "good" ones in a neat area and the rest would be cancelled.
- Instead of no time with her dog, she would take time to play with her beloved pet.
- Instead of feeling harried, she would feel calm, relaxed, and eager to work with her next client.

- Instead of too much work, she would set boundaries and limits on how many clients she accepted.

When Marshall woke up to the realization that retirement was not going to morph magically into his dream life, he thought, *What is wrong with this picture? Nothing is working the way I thought it would.* He remembered his early dreams before he retired. What could he do?

He jumped at the chance to attend a men's wilderness retreat where he knew the speaker would be talking about this topic. The speaker encouraged the men to spend time thinking about their lives and what they wanted to accomplish. The first step was to take time to think about how things would be if they were perfect.

While hiking through the surrounding woods, Marshall began thinking about what he really wanted to accomplish. He decided life would be perfect if he could:

- write some of his book every day
- have regular social time each week
- work with his grandchildren in his wood shop
- take the Spanish immersion class he had dreamed of for years
- plant a vegetable garden
- spend more time in the library
- join the church choir

On the Right Track

Without realizing it, each of these time-starved workers has in his or her own way taken what always has to be the first step in making change—they paused a moment on the treadmill to think about the present direction of their lives and what direction they want to go. None of them had a clue about how they would accomplish their dreams but the fact that they have dreamed at all is the door through which the solutions begin to march. In this book we offer ten practical how-tos of time management. The first and perhaps most important one is dream specifically about what you really, really want.

> **Time Management Choice #1**
>
> Dream big.

Perhaps you think that stopping to evaluate is a waste of the little time you have. Instead, you may want some quick tip or effective trick you can use to pour water on your burning time issues.

But it doesn't work that way. Time issues can't be solved without first stopping to evaluate and then to dream.

Nail It Down

Ideas drift. A burning, important goal today may turn to ashes tomorrow simply because we turn our attention to something else. We leave behind a trail of unrealized dreams. A Chinese proverb is that the weakest ink is better than the strongest memory. We will be smart to—drum roll, please—write it down!

A famous (though probably spurious) study from Yale in 1953 tells that the 3 percent of the Yale graduates who had written their goals while in college had more wealth years later than the other 97 percent combined. The validity of the study may be questioned but what is not in doubt is that taking up pen and making an effort to clarify your goals will give you a giant leap toward accomplishing them. To take full advantage of this powerful secret of how we can capture our dreams, we need to do three things with each goal:

1. Write it down specifically.

2. Attach a date you would like to see your dream achieved.
3. Look at it regularly, often, daily—in short, a lot.

If nothing stood in your way, what would your life be like? Or to put it another way, what would be a perfect life for you?

Your Sense of Purpose

Any life well lived must have an overall sense of purpose. When you ask yourself what would be the perfect life for you, you are really asking yourself, *What is my chief purpose in life and how can that work out in my practical everyday activities*? The closer our activities match our core beliefs and purpose, the more authentic our lives become.

As you read about different aspects of time management and consider making changes to upgrade your way of life, eventually you will ask yourself why you should care about changing. Once you know why you are concerned about your time, you are on the road to success. At that point you will want to write your own personal mission statement. In the last chapter of the book you will be reminded that you need to have a worthwhile focus in life, something that makes your life significant. That will be a good time to write a few sentences that reflect your raison d'être, the important reason or reasons you walk this earth. What footprints do you want to leave behind for others to follow?

As illustrated above, our use of time can spin out of control. The tension of a life out of sync with one's main purposes is what makes taking control important. Asking yourself, *What would my life be like if it were perfect*? helps to clarify what is really important to you. These chapters about time management will be important only as you apply them directly to yourself and your goals in life.

Forget the fact that you don't know at this time how your goals can be accomplished. Dream with abandon. Things seem to move toward the direction on which you concentrate. What is one issue involving your time that you would like to make perfect, that if you could change it today, you would? (Of course this applies to other kinds of goals as well, but we are focusing on time issues.) How would you make it perfect? There is probably more than one.

> Before the reality comes the dream.

The rest of this book will deal with how you can keep that focus and make your "perfect life" happen. Maintaining focus on the significant things in your life is a life-transforming experience. Sometimes having too many unnecessary things to do can make life feel just as cluttered as having too many things. In the next chapter we will discuss four dynamic methods for handling activity clutter.

Your Turn

☐ Using the list below, identify the things that are important in your life. Choose three or more you consider most important and write them down. Cross off or ignore those you have already accomplished or that you don't think are important.

1. Get home on time consistently.
2. Spend less time commuting.
3. Improve my work schedule.
4. Have fewer interruptions.
5. Complete projects on time without rushing.
6. Spend more time with my family.
7. Have more personal/private time for reading, prayer, thinking, and so on.
8. Sleep more/sleep regularly.

9. Exercise more consistently.
10. Get my paperwork done (and filed) efficiently.
11. Attend fewer meetings.
12. Spend more time with friends.
13. Have more vacation time.
14. Have more time for volunteer work/church.
15. Spend more time on household maintenance.
16. Spend less time looking for things.
17. Have time for mental improvement or study.
18. Travel more.
19. Enhance my spiritual life.
20. Go to school.
21. Other: _____

☐ Looking at the top three or more things that are important to your life, write a paragraph about each one. State
specifically how you would like to see that goal realized in
your life and, where appropriate, include a date or dates
as a target. Add a "payoff" sentence, so you can remind
yourself of the benefits of your goal. Here is an example:

Goal (some call it an objective): Get home on time consistently.

I want to start leaving the office as often as possible by
5:30 p.m. By January 1, I want to be able to do so four out of
five business days. To do this, I will . . . (add tactics here).
My payoff will be that I will have more time with the family
on a day-to-day basis and be more rested.

Once you have written your paragraphs, you need to focus
daily on your goals. Using a card for each, write with a bold
marker the top three goals and post them in a place you will
see them regularly. When one goal is reached, replace it with
the next in line. (More about how to keep up with your goals,
objectives, steps, and projects in chapters 10 and 11.) Some

people write goals on a card they carry around with them. The advantage of posting the cards is that they come into view when you aren't thinking about them, they are always visible, and you won't lose them.

If you wish, use your trusty computer in some way that keeps reminding you of your key goals.

Tips for Setting Goals

1. Make goals worthwhile. Make sure they are important enough to go after.
2. Choose goals you can envision. A very successful young man has a poster listing his life goals, and each has a picture beside it. One goal is "Have a college named after me," with a picture of a college beside it. We think it just might happen.
3. Decide on a time frame for accomplishing your goals.
4. Make your goals measurable so you can tell when you have reached them.
5. State each goal simply and clearly.
6. Tell others your goals so they can support your efforts.
7. Limit your goals to a few at a time.
8. Include your payoff to remind yourself of the reason you are going after this goal.

True or false?

1. I have trouble making decisions about what to do first.
2. I would like an easy way to prioritize my activities.
3. I like choices.

If you answered true to any of these, have we got a chapter for you!

---

5 handling activity clutter

four dynamic methods

Obstacles are those things we notice when we take our eyes off our goal.

Henry Ford

Creative people have more ideas and interests than any one person can do in a lifetime, and we accumulate the paraphernalia to prove it. If we're perfectionists, we may gather much more than we need for one activity, just in case. This chapter will introduce four possible approaches for handling activity clutter:

- Tournament format
- Priority quadrants
- Prioritize-your-to-do-list approach
- Streamlined to-do-list approach

Don't get hung up on which approach is the best. Pick the one you think is the simplest. If you don't like that one, go for another. Or jump around from time to time for variety. The important thing is to use a prioritizing system so you can decide how to begin an activity.

Not every activity is of equal value. Some of your ideas and interests are not worth your valuable time. They may be good ideas, inventive ideas, creative ideas—but they are not good enough for you to pursue *at this time*. Some of your ideas are dynamite and, if pursued, would change your life significantly for the better. But those great ideas, like diamonds among rocks, sometimes are lost in the mix when your life is cluttered.

> **Time Management Choice #2**
>
> Focus—keep the main thing the main thing.

Your job is to find the diamonds and lay aside or discard the rocks. Once you pinpoint those great ideas and begin to accomplish them in your life, you will notice a significant difference in the quality of your life and in your ability to achieve your life's dreams.

George Can't Decide

George could be a poster child for activity clutter. Sometime in his life, he got the erroneous idea that he could do it all. On a daily basis he swamps himself with activities he wants to pursue and when he thinks of something else that seems important, he tries to squeeze it in as well. As George tells it, these are the things he wants to do every day:

- Meditate twice a day.
- Exercise one half to one hour a day.
- Read a chapter from the Bible five times a day.
- Work on personal finances, budget records, financial newsletter, or care for his investments.
- Play the piano.
- Learn to speak Spanish.

- Learn French pronunciation.
- Iron pants, polish shoes, and care for other personal items.
- Work on his fourth step or cognitive behavioral therapy book or *What Color Is Your Parachute?*
- Plus other things like going to several association meetings a week, getting snagged for one to four hours of watching television, and journaling daily.

George wants to know how he can focus on his priority tasks, like:

- Reconciling his bank statements
- Catching up on entering his receipts in his budget program
- Caring for his investments
- Doing taxes
- Finding a job
- Decluttering his desk
- Painting rooms

He confesses a weakness for stopping to read anything on paper or the Web. He wants to know how he can get control of his life.

Obviously George is swamped, drowning in the quicksand of too many interests. He needs a strong hand to pull him out. George needs to step back and take a realistic look at his scheduling. Time management is not about getting everything done. Time management is about getting the most important things done; which means, time management is about making hard decisions concerning what is important. In short, for George, the strong hand needed is prioritizing.

In George's eyes everything is important. He is trying to be a modern-day Renaissance man and a Middle Ages scholar combined. And he is unrealistically passionate about it all. He needs an approach that will cull out the least important activities so he will have time to do the important ones. The tournament format below is a good method for him because it simplifies his choices down to only two things at a time.

The Tournament Format

The tournament format, which eliminates the weaker opponent and arrives at a champion, fits George's needs perfectly. In this approach the person makes a vertical list of the top sixteen things that need to be done. Then grouping them by twos (that is 1 and 2 together, 3 and 4 together, and so on), the person begins choosing which of the two items in the couplet is the most important to do, continuing to pare the list down until the four most important tasks remain.

You may find this method a good one for you. Use a chart like the one below. As your choices are narrowed, you will

Tournament Format

1.
2.
3.
4.
5.
6.
7.
8.
9.
10.
11.
12.
13.
14.
15.
16.

close in on what your real priority activities are. Slowly, what is important rises to the surface.

Priority Quadrants

The priority quadrant method is said to have been used by President Dwight Eisenhower, and Stephen Covey has popularized it.

A square is divided into four quadrants and each activity is written in a quadrant, depending on how important and how urgent it is. "Important" relates to the impact the item would have if it were not done. "Urgent" relates to whether there is a time deadline. The four quadrants are:

1. *Urgent and important.* Activities that are important and urgent will be done immediately, because they are not optional. Sometimes these are unavoidable, as in an accident or illness. Sometimes they could have been avoided if the person had been proactive and solved problems before they became urgent.

   If a water hose breaks in the basement, it immediately becomes a crisis. The condition of the rotting hose was always important but now the situation has become urgent because we neglected it. If we find ourselves repeatedly putting out fires, it is a wake-up call to manage our lives better. Perhaps we are causing crises by procrastinating or not being proactive.

   Quadrant 1 is the quadrant of crisis.
2. *Not urgent but important.* This is the most powerful quadrant, the quadrant of life quality. The items in this quadrant relate to things that would enhance our lives tremendously if they were attended to regularly. However, because they are not urgent, they are easy to neglect. This quadrant is the heart of personal time management.

In this quadrant lives the book we always wanted to write or the business we always wanted to start. Here we see all of the things that would make our lives better, if we only did them. But often we let them slide, because they do not have a time deadline. These include family time, reading to your three-year-old, planting a garden, exercising, volunteering, and many other activities you feel are important to who you are.

Pick and use time management systems and tools to keep the items in this quadrant alive and well (see chapters 16, 17, 18). Spotlight them and give them a completion date. Otherwise they will slowly die in the graveyard of forgetfulness and neglect.

3. *Urgent but not important*. This is the quadrant where we are responding to the tyranny of the urgent. We may stop something important that we are doing to answer the phone, go to a scheduled meeting, talk to a drop-in interrupter, or answer incoming email.

None of these may be important, but we handle them because they have a degree of time urgency to them. Often these tasks can be delegated or modified so they don't interrupt the important things.

4. *Not urgent and not important*. This is the relaxation quadrant. This is what the water cooler concept is all about. People want to have an excuse to take a break, stretch their legs, and refresh themselves. Television and computer games are in this area. The problem comes when this quadrant is overused. Items here can be dropped without causing problems.

Like all busy working moms, Joan was overrun with multiple activities that related to home and business. Her activities all jumbled together and were separated only by the clock that put her at her work. She had jobs like signing school papers, writing work reports, picking up a child from tumbling, creating a budget at work, paying the tax bill, faxing invitations to a meeting, writing personal thank-you notes, and checking employee time sheets.

Joan was overburdened because she gave the same priority weight to all the items on her to-do list. She just listed them one by one in a column and checked them off as she got to them.

Joan started using the quadrant method to try to bring some order to her daily activities, depending on their importance. She drew a big plus on her paper, separating the sheet into four squares. In the upper left-hand quadrant she wrote the words, "Urgent and important." Then she looked through her list for all the jobs that should be written in that quadrant. Paying the tax bill and signing the school permission slip were included in quadrant 1.

In quadrant 2 (not urgent but important), she included some really important things that could be very helpful in securing a promotion. Over and above the call of duty, she decided to suggest to her boss that she design the layout for the new newsletter the boss was writing. That would enable her to work more closely with the boss, but it was not a long-term commitment. So she wrote this in quadrant 2.

She also decided to write thank-you cards on behalf of her department to the members of the building improvement committee that had led in the recent office redecoration. At home she wanted to design and create a new holiday candle centerpiece for the table. She wrote all of these in quadrant 2. They were not urgent but they would eventually enhance her life.

In quadrant 3 (urgent but not important) she wrote things like replacing her old credit card with the new one she had been sent and changing her doctor's appointment.

Joan liked quadrant 4 (not urgent and not important) the best. They were her fun items, like putting calligraphy on the bottom of an invitation she is designing, watching the rest of the Dr. Phil show she had taped, and checking personal email.

Putting the items she needed to do in quadrants helped her see that she had been spending a lot of time on things that were not really priorities.

Urgent/Not Urgent Quadrants

	Urgent	Not Urgent
Important	**I** Urgent & Important	**II** Not Urgent & Important
Not Important	**III** Urgent & Not Important	**IV** Not Urgent & Not Important

The Prioritize-Your-To-Do-List Approach

The to-do list is the workhorse of daily productivity. (More will be said about it in chapter 12.) It is the perfect place to start prioritizing daily activities and sorting out the clutter. First, you need to tame your long list of activities by placing them in four corrals. Divide a paper into four squares by drawing a line from top to bottom and from side to side in the center of the page. It starts out looking like the four-quadrant method above but it uses an entirely different approach and labeling.

Label each square with the words Do, Call, Go (errands), and Buy (things outside of work). From your long list choose the ones you want to do the next day and place them in the appropriate squares—about six in each. Grouping activities in this way is wonderfully different from the usual long list that includes everything you have to do. Only by trying it can a person realize its power. When you group tasks in this way, you find several that you can do together, and this saves time—like making several phone calls or doing several errands to the same part of town. Place a star beside the most important item in each group as a guide to where to start.

Of course, you can put the four divisions on a list on your computer and color each division a different color. As each task is completed, cross it out, put it in italics, or delete it.

Go/Call/Do/Buy Quadrants

Go	Call
1.	1.
2.	2.
3.	3.
4.	4.
5.	5.
6.	6.
Do	**Buy**
1.	1.
2.	2.
3.	3.
4.	4.
5.	5.
6.	6.

A Streamlined To-Do-List Approach

In the annals of management history, the best-known story about time management involves Charles Schwab, president of Bethlehem Steel, and Ivy Lee, a consultant. Schwab asked Lee how he could get more done with his time. Lee handed Schwab a piece of paper and told him to write down the most important tasks he needed to do the next day in their order of importance. He told Schwab, "Do them in order, not going to the next one until the first is complete. Don't worry if you don't get them all done in one day. Just stay at each job to full completion." Lee added that if it worked for him, he should share it with his employees. He said Schwab could pay him what it was worth.

Sometime later Lee received a check for twenty-five thousand dollars, a very large sum in the l930s.

This easy-to-use and intuitive method is beautiful in its simplicity and power because it spotlights what is really significant. You will find that as you use this method your progress may not flow as smoothly as you might hope. Give yourself permission to modify this system by shifting their order as circumstances require. Occasionally you may find that a goal is not really a priority or that it has become obsolete with time or circumstances. Sometimes the progress of one goal gets stuck and you jump to another until you can move forward on the first.

The important focus is to keep the main things the main thing. Be aware that things of lesser importance may never get done. Knowing that is one of the keys to successful time management. Remember that time management is not the art of getting everything done. It is the art of getting the most important things done. To put it another way, it is priority management.

Pareto's Principle

Alfredo Pareto, an Italian economist, discovered an economic principle that has since been applied to many areas of life— the 80/20 rule. His basic premise was that only a small portion (about 20 percent) of any group is really significant.

Applied to your many activities, this theory postulates that only a few are really important to be done. In fact 20 percent of your activities will account for the bulk (80 percent) of your effectiveness. This chapter on priorities has described four different methods to help you find those significant few activities—to find the diamonds among the stones.

When you choose your important activities, lesser ones fall to the bottom of the list. Many of the activities that did not make the cut are still important and perhaps can be done sometime in the future.

When you get to the chapters on project management (chapters 10 and 11), you will find a way to conserve those good ideas, which clears them out of your life for now but saves them for possible use in the future.

Once you have chosen your true priorities, you can begin to work on them in ways that we will describe later. But for now, pat yourself on the back for your success in sorting out all the activities of your life.

Once you know what you really want to do, it is time to open your eyes to what you are actually doing on a regular basis. Does what you do jibe with what you should be doing? The next chapter will help you decide.

Your Turn

Choose the method for prioritizing your activities that seems best for you.

☐ Experiment until you find the method that works. You may vary them according to your need from time to time. Any one of them will give you the tools you need to isolate your most important activities.

☐ Once you identify your priorities (those 20 percent that produce 80 percent of your results), it is important that you spotlight them. You can do this by scheduling them at a particular time on your paper or computer planner instead of leaving them on your to-do list where they may remain indefinitely.

☐ If you prefer to work directly from your to-do list, you can designate them with A (top priority) activities, B (less important), or C (least important). Do As and Bs first. Cs may be deferred indefinitely, may never get done, or are delegated to someone else to do.

☐ Name the method you like best.

Tips

1. Make your activities count. Set goals before you decide what to do.
2. Every week try to do one thing that will bring you closer to your long-term goals.
3. Repeatedly ask yourself, *Am I doing the most productive or important thing right now?*
4. Do only what takes you toward your goal.
5. Remember Pareto's principle. Focus your attention and effort on the all-important 20 percent.

Yes or no?

1. Have you ever kept a log of your time?
2. Have you done it recently?
3. Are you willing to keep a log to evaluate your personal productivity?

If you answered no to questions 1 and 2 and yes to question 3, you are ready to take a giant leap forward.

---

6 measure your time

keep a time log

I don't need more time. I need a deadline!

Duke Ellington

If you want to begin to lose weight, write down what you eat as you eat it. It will be a real eye-opener. If you want to work on your finances, keep a record of where your money is going. You'll soon see spending habits that need to change. If you want to be a better manager of your time, keep track of how you use the hours of your day. You'll be amazed at how easy it is to waste time.

Management theorist Peter Drucker has repeatedly said that if you can't measure it, you can't manage it. Certainly the use of time can be measured, managed, and made better.

Bev Gets an Eye-Opener

Bev is a busy mom who never has enough time because of family interruptions. Her children and husband rely on her to take up the slack when they have time management problems, which are often caused by their lack of preparation. Things that are important to Bev are falling by the wayside because she is busy helping everyone else. She and her sister wanted to plan a family reunion but she has not been able to schedule in the planning time. Fondly she remembers when she used to read a novel a month but she can't remember the last time she read a book. She would like to plan and prepare nutritious meals on a weekly basis, but often she must whip up something quick a half hour before mealtime. *Where does the time go?* she wonders.

Taking a piece of paper, she writes the days of the week across the top and the hours of the day down the side.

She decides she will set her kitchen timer for an hour and at the end of the hour she will note what she has done during that time. She isn't going to make a big job out of keeping track but she is curious to see what she can learn by looking realistically at how she uses her time.

At the end of the week, Bev notices that her days are filled with petty interruptions. She knew that of course, but now she can see more clearly how this happens.

First, she notices that often her five-year-old daughter calls on her for help with some need: money for ice cream, to reach a toy, to clean up a spill. When her thirteen-year-old son gets home from school, he wants her to find things for him and help with his schoolwork. Often her husband asks her for small favors. Phone calls come from family and friends at various times during the day.

Being no dummy, she comes up with a plan that makes sense for her time use.

- For her daughter, she sets up a system of easily accessed shelves with a jar holding change for the ice cream vendor, toys that are easy to get out (and put back), and a few simple first-aid supplies. She puts pictures on the front of the shelves so the little girl knows where the items can be found.

- She makes a study area for her son, stocked with supplies. Each day she lets him know when she will be available to help him with his work.
- She asks her husband what he anticipates his needs might be for the next day. If he needs a shirt ironed or some other favor, she wants to do it the night before.

She helps when necessary but slowly pulls back from her family's dependence on her. Above her kitchen desk she posts a sign: "Lack of preparation on your part does not necessarily constitute an emergency on my part." When her family has to solve the problems they have created and clean up their own messes (literal and otherwise), they become more careful not to create avoidable problems. As a result, Bev is able to tune back into the family without fear of being bombarded by unnecessary demands.

Bev bought a planner and writes various activities on it, including planning the reunion with her sister and reading for pleasure. She starts working on a three-week circulating menu. When she begins planning ahead for meals, she can cook double portions and freeze the extras. She makes a rule about laundry: she will do only as much as she can start and have put away by the end of the day. Finally, she groups activities she can do together. For example, she screens her calls and returns those left on her answering machine all at once.

Without saying anything, these slight changes in behavior telegraph loud and clear a change in Bev's attitude. As she begins to value her time, she realizes she can do much more for her family, assuming the role of a responsible adult instead of a useful helper. It is certainly a more satisfying way of life for her.

Cheryl, the Office Helper

Cheryl is a well-organized legal assistant for two busy attorneys. Often she will be working on a project for one attorney and be interrupted by the second with an urgent request to do something important for him. She handled it well and even enjoyed juggling her projects. It kept her from being bored. Everyone was happy until another attorney's assistant quit and Cheryl was the designated pinch hitter for him as well.

Her organizational systems could not cope with the overload and began to crumble. What was she going to do? To bring some clarity to the situation, she began to keep track of her activities using a simple time log.

She listed all the things she did each day for a week. Every half hour she jotted down most of what she did, though it was sometimes hard to remember it all.

At the end of the week she reviewed the chart and was amazed to see the pattern of her work. Using three different color highlighters, she marked the work for each attorney. She saw how she was jumping from one project to another randomly. Now she saw the problem.

To clarify her work, she kept each attorney's paperwork in a different colored folder. She also continued to keep a time log indicating the project she was on and for whom. She now endeavored to finish each project before going to the next. For her own sake, she continued to color the time log with the highlighter. While this approach did not lessen her work, it brought a sense of order to her daily activities.

Bev and Cheryl are somewhat alike in that they were both interrupted by other people's needs. Bev wanted to give her attention to other things like reading. Cheryl woke up to the fact that she needed to direct her work differently for her job's sake. Both used the time log to see their situation clearly and realize what they could do to change it.

Mel, the Lone Concrete Ranger

Mel was an independent sales rep for a concrete manufacturing company, making sales by contacts in person and by phone. He works from home because he is responsible for opening a new territory. After an on-site visit to evaluate the needs, Mel writes up a proposal at his office and returns to the site with the information.

Now that he has left his previous corporate office, where his schedule was prearranged, Mel is having trouble getting in gear. Sometimes it is two o'clock before he phones the first prospect. He realizes this is economic suicide. If he does not start making sales in the new territory, he could get fired. Or worse, he might have to return to the corporate office as a failure. As a desperate measure, Mel begins a time log.

When he evaluates his time log, he is appalled to see how little time he has worked. *Yikes*, he thinks. *This is worse than I thought*. He decides to "act as if" he were in the corporate office. By eight o'clock he is dressed and heads for his home office. At nine o'clock he starts making his first call and continues till noon when he allows himself to go on the Internet to check his mail. On days when he does not have an appointment, he begins research at two o'clock to locate more prospects. This whole approach failed miserably for Mel until another lone ranger from the company shared his own personal insight and remedy for working alone.

It was this. People have different styles. Some people are compartmentalizers who are able to go easily from one task to another and enjoy variety. Other people have trouble switching. Once they begin a job, they prefer to stick with it all day. They need to schedule groups of tasks by the day.

Mel had trouble switching from one task to another. Once he realized that he dreaded the compartmentalized approach of phone calls in the morning and on-site visits in the afternoon, he changed. He preferred scheduling calls all day Monday, on-site visits all day Tuesday, writing proposals on Wednesday, revisiting sites with proposals or research on Thursday, and doing paperwork and correspondence on Friday. With his new approach he enjoyed working from home and was successful.

Careful Scrutiny

Often, just looking at your time log is enough to let you know where you need to change. If, however, you need to scrutinize the things your log reveals, you can highlight different activities in different colors. For example, highlight all your interruptions in red, meetings in green, phone calls in yellow, and so on. This will give you a better visual picture of how you spend your time. Identify the time when you are not being productive. These times need to be diminished and more time needs to be spent on your priorities.

Don't make keeping a time log more work than it needs to be. It shouldn't be complex and time-consuming. Keeping track on a simple time log for a limited time can spotlight the activities that are filling up your day and allows you to evaluate if those activities are the most important ways to use your time.

Some people who like to quantify facts can evaluate what percentage of time is spent in various areas. This can be an eye-opening activity.

Doing more than one thing at a time is one way to multiply your use of time. The next chapter tells how this method can be useful but also how it can get you into trouble.

Your Turn

☐ Using a time log like the one below, keep track of how you use your time for a week. Highlight interruptions.

☐ Evaluate where your use of time is off track and make the changes you see are needed.

Time Log   Day_____ Date_____

6 AM	
6:30	
7	
7:30	
8	
8:30	
9	
9:30	
10	
10:30	
11	
11:30	
12 Noon	
12:30	
1	
1:30	
2	
2:30	
3	
3:30	
4	
4:30	
5	
5:30	
6 PM	
6:30	
7	
7:30	
8	
8:30	

Tips

1. Keep track of where your time goes on a time log. Don't put it off.
2. Write on your time log every half hour—don't wait till the end of the day to try and remember what you've done.
3. You can use a log both for work and for home. It can even help you make good use of your leisure time.
4. Try using different colors on your time log to segment the various types of activities you worked on.
5. Keep it simple. Don't use your time log as a substitute for a journal.

Yes or no?

1. Does having a lot of irons in the fire stimulate you?
2. Do you sometimes forget where you are in your projects?
3. Is your life controlled to a large degree by the needs of others?

If you answered yes to two of the three above, your lively and helpful life needs a little guidance. Give careful consideration to when to turn on the steam and when to slow down and focus.

---

7 modern multitasking

help and hindrance

> I say, let your affairs be as two or three, and not a hundred
> or a thousand; instead of a million count half a dozen, and
> keep your accounts on your thumbnail.
>
> A man is rich in proportion to the number of things which
> he can afford to let alone.
>
> Henry David Thoreau

Moderns, for the most part, love multitasking. It is stimulating
and makes us feel powerful. But somewhere deep down we
may feel a little uncomfortable about it. We may sense that
doing so much may not always be good for us.

If you feel this way, you are right. It is stimulating to have
several things going at once but it is not always good for us.
Let's look at how this works out in today's world in several
different types of multitasking.

Maryanne—Many Things at Once

Maryanne is a classic multitasker. She takes a clipboard everywhere she goes and always sports a cell phone earpiece. She

makes sure she carries a supply of informational pamphlets and ads relating to her nurse-practitioner business. As she strides across the hospital campus, she leafs through new material she has received, makes notes, places calls, and maybe eats her sandwich. With pride she jokes that she can eat lunch, make calls, and exercise by walking, all at the same time. Unfortunately, she is not really "there" for each of her activities. She doesn't enjoy or even remember all of the things she has done, what she had for lunch, all that was said during her conversations, or the weather as she walked. She also doesn't realize the level of stress her habit of multitasking is creating.

Technology has brought the opportunity to overdo into all of our lives. It forces on us a conscious decision on how to use, or not use, the over-the-top technology available today. Too much availability is drowning many people in opportunities to do more than they can handle. Though it is exhilarating in its own way, often it's removing the flavor from life.

Maryanne misses out on how good the sandwich tastes or how beautiful the sky is. In short she is missing out on the texture of life, while stressing out her health as well. She vows to start taking it easy and stop the frenetic pace of her life, but habits are usually hard to break.

Jennifer—Jumping from One Task to Another

Jennifer loves to multitask. She believes that by doing two or three things at once she is getting more done, but in reality projects are often uncompleted because she is trying to do too much at once. When she does finish something, it is usually in a last-minute rush. Explaining her rationale she says, "I like having several things going at once. It keeps me from being bored."

Some people have an adrenaline addiction. Jennifer is one. She allows her projects to get to the point where she must rush them to completion. Finishing a task at the last minute is like winning a race. Pulling it off with no time to spare is exhilarating.

Jennifer feels that she does her best creative work under pressure. This approach has become a habit with her, but she complains about the time pressures that have become a way of life. Unfortunately, studies show that work actually suffers from last-minute preparation. What's more, Jennifer's frenetic approach is not good for her health. It is healthier for her job and her body if projects are completed well and with less stress. If she continues with her present way of doing things, she may begin to suffer from excitement burnout and will no longer be able to stimulate that same rush that currently carries her forward.

David—Forced Confusion

David has lots of work to do. He is in charge of intake in the reception area of a local community center. His job is to handle the phone and paperwork for walk-in clients who are applying for social services. His biggest frustration comes when he is working with a person at the window and the phone rings. Who comes first? Unlike Jennifer, he hates having to switch from one task to another. Competing demands are the bane of all front desk workers.

When David asked his boss who should have priority, the people on the phone or the people at the reception window, his boss sidestepped the issue and told him they were both priorities. So David decided to make a plan. To avoid the strain of trying to do too many things at once, he decided to handle the people at the window first, taking phone calls as he had a break from clients in the window line. Later he set aside time to go to voice mail and return calls he had missed earlier. He did most of his paperwork with each client and closed his window for a half hour at the end of his day to do the necessary filing.

Analyzing Multitasking

Maryanne, Jennifer, and David are trying to multitask, handle more than one activity in a short period of time. This can cause problems. According to an article by Joshua Rubenstein and David Meyer in the *Journal of Experimental Psychology*, switching from one task to another actually wastes time. Two separate preparatory thought processes take place when switching tasks. First, you must decide to switch to a different task: *I think I will stop this and instead do that*. Second, when you switch to a new task, you need to reorient yourself. You must think, *What is this all about? Where am I in the process? What needs to be done next?* All of this mental stopping and starting takes time and energy.

Rubenstein and Meyer also report that multitasking can actually harm the individual who makes it a way of life. Because of stress hormones that flood the brain, multitasking can result in short-term memory loss. Short-term memory loss caused by stress hormones that attack the memory area of the brain can eventually become a permanent condition.

Making the Choice

To multitask or not to multitask, that is the question—as we think again of words of Shakespeare (sort of). Multitasking flows like electricity into all of our lives. Let's be honest. Switching from one activity to another can be very beneficial under certain circumstances. We even enjoy it to a certain degree because it makes us feel powerful and it helps us get a lot done. At times we all will do it, no matter what the research says may be the result. So we need to know when it is okay and when we should avoid it.

People vary and are complex. However, in general, men tend to compartmentalize their thinking into segmented boxes and, if they multitask, they do it within one box. Women tend to be more flexible and jump from box to box in their thinking, so their multitasking is more diverse.

Don't Overdo

Maryanne, the one who walked across the hospital campus eating and talking on her phone, appears to be doing several things simultaneously. In reality, she is not. She is shifting her concentration back and forth from one activity to another so quickly that the shift is undetectable. Attending to several projects at one time like Maryanne or jumping deliberately from one task to another like Jennifer are two forms of multitasking prevalent in the modern world among active people.

A certain amount of simple multitasking is normal and enjoyable, but humans can't really attend successfully to several *simple* tasks at once or to two *complex* activities at one time. Thus, examples of unwise multitasking are talking on a cell phone while driving, watching television while studying, or texting a friend while listening to a lecture in class.

Multitasking is more involved than it appears. What Maryanne and Jennifer are actually doing is making a series of executive decisions about which activity to attend to as they address several things in rapid-fire sequence. All of this toggling back and forth while engaging in two high-level, complex activities is counterproductive and stressful for most individuals.

Benign Multitasking

While trying to do two demanding and complex activities at once is stressful, multitasking while doing mindless activities is another story. Listening to the radio while driving, chewing gum while walking, and folding towels while watching television are three illustrations of simple tasks that we can all do easily at the same time. Mothers are legendary multitaskers, jumping from one interrupted activity to another to meet the needs of their children. And usually they can do this without any detrimental results, except for exhaustion at the end of the day.

Sometimes linking two tasks can be beneficial. Often we suggest that people listen to enjoyable music while doing a boring job like filing or listen to an audio book during cleaning. The desire to hear the next episode of the story during cleaning can bring us back enthusiastically to the undesirable, boring task. In these cases, one noncomplex enjoyable activity (listening) is being married to one boring activity (cleaning or filing). This multitasking helps us get the unpleasant job done.

Multiplanning

People who get a lot done with more ease than others have learned a key to success. They multiplan. They sandwich activities together that can be logically joined. For example, when heading down the hall, they take a pair of shoes left in the living room to drop off in the bedroom. When going out to lunch, they take their paycheck by the bank they pass on the way.

Multiplanning requires a kind of casual memory (sometimes called scratch memory) for what needs to be done so that when an appropriate opportunity comes up, we are ready. One of the characteristics of successful multiplanners is that they are alert to how things can fit easily together. They have a workable mental (or written) list of what needs to be done and they are constantly piggybacking one thing onto another, while their time-harried friends, who do not multiplan, stand in awe of how much they get done.

With planning we can creatively and successfully do many things together to our benefit. We can group activities and we can sandwich activities. When there is down time or waiting time in our day, which there often is, we can be alert and prepared, having a readily available, working to-do list, listing activities we can sandwich in between our larger projects. For example, while you are on hold with customer service of some company, you can put your phone on speaker and fold clothes. When waiting for someone to arrive for an appointment, you can check your emails or draft a letter. It's always good to have an additional task planned when you have extra time.

Taking Control

Sensible multiplanning is almost always beneficial. However, it is not always clear when its cousin, multitasking, is beneficial or when it should be avoided. With so many opportunities and so much instant and portable communication available, often we open ourselves to questionable multitasking that needs to be evaluated and may need to be moderated.

Life does not come at us in compartmentalized boxes. It comes in bits and pieces. The better we learn to manage these pieces, to fit them together in a sensible way, the more we will get done with less strain and more time to spare.

If we are able to manage it well, fitting the pieces together can be beneficial. But it is easy to develop a way of life in which multitasking gets out of hand and needs to be controlled. The multitaskers we have met in this chapter need to make adjustments.

1. Maryanne should make a conscious effort not to attempt two complex activities at once. As a beginning, she needs to honor her own personal needs by taking time out for lunch.
2. Jennifer must prioritize one or two projects and see each one as far as she can before switching to another. Don't start new projects until you have caught up on the backlog of those already started.

3. David needs to stick to his decision to prioritize his clients. He developed a plan that he would attend to one person at a time and concentrate fully on that person until he was finished. Once he sees how well this works he will be confirmed in his commitment and develop the authoritative attitude needed to enforce it.

Helpful Multitasking

Multitasking of simple activities, rightly done, is great. It helps us to do more and it keeps us energized and productive. But be careful about trying to do too many things, especially complex things, at one time. Even the best juggler has a limit to how many balls he can successfully keep in the air at once.

Commit to focusing on completing one complex task at a time whenever possible. When doing simple activities, make it a point to focus on and really appreciate what is going on in your life. Savoring life is more important than the frenzy of runaway multitasking. Don't be so busy keeping your balls in the air that you can't relate to the world around you.

The moral of the story is: doing several things at once is often useful and makes us feel powerful, but be careful not to overdo, lowering the quality of your work and devaluing the moments of your life.

Another characteristic of life that can become toxic if overdone is the desire to do things well, too well. We will address the topic of perfectionism next.

Your Turn

☐ Make a list of the times and types of activities during which you consistently multitask.

☐ Would you benefit from:

- limiting the number of activities you try to do at the same time?
- prioritizing activities so that you don't have more than one or two big jobs "on the table" at once?

Tips

1. Procrastinate productively by having another important task waiting when you get bogged down on the first one.
2. It's okay to do more than one mindless task at a time.
3. Become sensitive to how many tasks you can have "in the works" at one time without getting confused or frustrated.
4. When doing one major task, take mental breaks by working on a smaller task. But never lose sight of your priority job.
5. At the end of the day, put everything away. Don't leave several projects out to get back to tomorrow.
6. Make notes often (on a sticky note) to remind yourself where you left off in a project.

Yes or no?

1. Do you consider yourself a perfectionist?
2. Does perfectionism in some areas hinder your progress in others?
3. Do you often apply the slogan "Do it right or not at all" to your activities?

If you answered yes to any of the above, you are to be congratulated on your strong desire to do things just right. But watch out that this tendency doesn't keep you from using your time as wisely as you could. Read on.

---

8 perfectionism

helpful or harmful?

Done is better than perfect.

Messies Anonymous
Twelve-Step slogan

Usually perfectionism has to do with how the details of a project are handled. A project done with the details appropriately handled is a wonderful thing. It is a great feeling to put away the final tool used in a completed building project, so is submitting on time a finished report. While most of us consider it very important to accomplish a task well and on time, perfectionists become tangled up in how to apply this concept.

Sheila—Agonizing over Details

Sheila's graphic design business was losing clients because she didn't get her designs to her customers on time. She agonized over every minute detail, sometimes spending hours choosing an appropriate font, rearranging placements, and tweaking ideas. Her workmanship was meticulous, and those who knew her work said her pieces were ready for the client long before she was ready to deliver them. Afraid the product was not as perfect as she could make it, she found it almost impossible to say it was finished.

Sheila is a classic rigid perfectionist. Although she has heard the expression "Done is better than perfect" and has seen the admonition on the bumper sticker that says, "Just do it!" she is plagued by her desire to do it just a little bit better. Somehow it does not occur to her that not delivering the product when it is needed is the most imperfect thing she could do.

Misplaced perfectionism like Sheila's is a common hindrance in project completion. Failure to complete a project is often the result of giving attention to details that do not matter significantly while neglecting the overall goal of the project, which does matter.

Sheila needs to get her perfectionism under control by setting certain guidelines:

1. Let someone else evaluate when the work is done.
2. Give herself a time deadline.
3. Allow only a predetermined number of revisions.

Joan and Patty—Indecision

Rigid perfectionism is consistently detrimental in the area of decision making. Joan wanted to go on a wonderful cruise with her husband for their fortieth wedding anniversary. All of the brochures looked so good that she could not decide which was best. The anniversary came and went without the cruise, and they have never gotten back to the plan. Choosing any one of the reputable cruise lines would have been better than no decision at all.

Patty had similar choices to make. She was in charge of locating a facility for the office Christmas party. Determined to do a superior job, she spent hours, many on her own time, visiting venues. She considered the decor, the distance, the cost, the location, the dates available, and many other details so that she could locate the very best place and impress the boss. Unfortunately, she spent so much time weighing the unweighable that she had to accept an unsatisfactory location for the party at an undesirable time because the others were booked while she was trying to decide.

One way Joan and Patty could have handled their indecision would have been to pass the top three possibilities on to somebody else and let that person make the decision. Joan's husband and Patty's boss could have made the final choice.

Don't give more attention than necessary to details while neglecting the overall goal. If you can't make a final decision, hand it off to somebody who can.

Philosophical Perfectionism

Undoubtedly the single most daunting and difficult problem to overcome is philosophical perfectionism. Rooted in fear, it is the attitude that "I must avoid a mistake at all costs." In the illustrations above, fear of making a mistake paralyzed a satisfactory completion of an important project.

Sometimes fear of failure keeps people from even beginning a project. Fred often said he had "two books up here," pointing to his head, but he never started writing because he didn't want to botch it up. Genevieve didn't make her bed because she could never do it well enough to meet her high standards. Ironing was always excruciating for Morgan as she chased down every little wrinkle. Olivia did not discard any financial papers because she was afraid she might need them later. With the resulting huge pile of papers, she could never locate the important ones. In the same way, she had so many phone numbers in her PDA, it was a task locating a specific one.

Sometimes perfectionistic behavior is encouraged from childhood when parents repeat a ditty that is good when rightly used but often misapplied by perfectionists.

> If a task is once begun,
> Never leave it till it is done.
> Be the labor great or small,
> Do it well or not at all.

Since perfectionists have an unreasonable concept of what doing it "well" is, they are tempted not to do it at all. And often, as with the unmade bed, they don't.

Philosophical perfectionists can benefit from playing a powerfully effective mind game. They say to themselves, *Of course I can't write this book* (or whatever), *but if I could, I would make an outline like this.* Then move on to: *Of course I can't write an outline for a book, but if I could, what are the top ten points I'd like to make?* And continue to: *Of course I can't write nine or ten things, but if I could, the first one I would write is . . .*

Too High a Price

Some perfectionists, like Fred and Genevieve, are afraid to start; others don't know when to stop. They relate to the part of the ditty that says, "Never leave it till it is done." They have difficulty knowing what "done" looks like. Sometimes they reach the goal, but they have paid an unreasonable price.

Pastor Nick neglected other pastoral duties and his family to spend hours on his sermons each week. Amber drove herself to exhaustion by overly preparing for teaching her class of special needs students. Both are in danger of burning themselves out or seriously limiting their goals in other areas of their lives.

Once you realize that you find it difficult to know when good enough is good enough, it is beneficial to involve someone else in the process, someone who can give you dispassionate feedback about your work and remind you about your need to stop or about a previously agreed on time schedule.

Just do it!

Reasonable Perfectionism

Strive for dedication to high quality work but remember to keep a balance of your overall goals in mind. If you find you are neglecting important areas by concentrating on one, if you are not getting your work done because your standards are unrealistic, or if you are accomplishing goals at an unreasonably high price because you are rigidly perfectionistic, make an effort to break out of that mind-set. The following thought will send shivers down the spines of true perfectionists. Here it is: In most cases, good enough really is good enough.

What to Do about It

If you have perfectionistic tendencies, all is not lost. You can challenge those tendencies and learn to put your time to better use. Here are some suggestions.

- Commit yourself to getting a job done by a certain time and then quitting at that time. Don't allow yourself to go over it "one last time."
- Be clear about what you want to accomplish and don't allow yourself to do more than you have decided at the beginning.

- If you find yourself endlessly fine-tuning, revising, and tinkering with a project, you need to realize that this is often a way to avoid completing it. Are you afraid of being judged on your completed project, or are you reluctant to show someone else up?

- When working on a project, it is important to remain objective and not mix your personal esteem with how the project is done. You can do this by remembering that you are a human *being* not a human *doing*.

- Create a false deadline that you take seriously so you won't work up to the very last minute and thus you will be finished on time.

- Involve others in evaluating your work as you go along. Accept their feedback as an indication of how much work still needs to be done.

- Keep a balance of activities, being careful not to overdo in one area and neglect others. For example, leave your work at the office so that when you get home, you are able to spend time with your family.

- Be willing to look for an easier or faster way to do something, even if it may not seem as good. For example, try putting dishes into the dishwasher without first rinsing them. Check to see if they don't come out as clean as when they have been rinsed first.

- As a challenge to your perfectionism, allow yourself to do something poorly on purpose. For example, leave wrinkles in your bed, set the table with the silverware in the wrong places or not aligned, send a personal email with a misspelled word. You will begin to realize that the world doesn't come to an end just because you didn't do some task perfectly.

Wanting to do things perfectly is one of the reasons for procrastination, which will be discussed in the next chapter.

Your Turn

☐ Name three projects you are working on or want to begin.

☐ Set a date for finishing each one. and commit yourself to finishing on schedule even if the finished projects do not meet your standard of perfection.

Look through the list above of things you can do to challenge your perfectionistic tendencies. Choose two or three to begin incorporating into your daily life.

Tips

1. Remember, only God is perfect. We are mere mortals.
2. Don't keep redoing or improving completed work. Move on.
3. Establish a point of completion and, once there, stop.
4. Just make your systems good enough to work; don't make them perfect.
5. Work toward a deadline, not toward perfection.

Yes or no?

1. Are things often left out because you do not put them back quickly?
2. Do you deal with emergencies that develop because you failed to take action earlier?
3. Do you tend to procrastinate because you know you don't have time to do something correctly?

If you answered yes to any of the above, keep reading.

---

9 procrastination

overcoming a nonproductive tendency

Hard work is often the easy work you did not do at the proper time.

Bernard Meltzer

Putting off an easy thing makes it hard, and putting off a hard one makes it impossible.

George H. Lonmer

Laura is busy. She knows her car has gone more than four thousand miles since her last oil change. But surely, it can wait a little longer. Fred's dentist keeps sending him a bill for his last visit. He knows he should pay it. But surely, it can wait a little longer. After Renée's friend's wallet was stolen, he begged her to make copies of all of her credit cards and ID cards so she would be prepared in case the same thing happened to her. She knows she ought to. But surely, it can wait a little longer.

Sound familiar? If procrastination is part of your life, coming to terms with it will be like lifting a heavy rock from your chest. What a relief!

There are two aspects to procrastination. First, there is the time-related type of procrastinating. It occurs when you have identified any task that is both important and is becoming urgent, as time for its completion comes, and you still don't do it. Filing your income tax return or turning in a report are examples.

Time Management Choice #3
Do it now!

There is another type of procrastination that is very destructive when it becomes chronic. In a household setting it may be packages dropped at the door, newspapers left on the floor, a roll of toilet paper left on the vanity rather than put on the dispenser, dishes left in the sink, and the like.

In a business setting we have known workers who pile rather than file, who don't return commonly used items, who don't work in a timely fashion by not returning phone calls, sending emails, gathering important facts, or preparing monthly financial records.

Procrastination is the vampire of productive living. It can suck the energy out of any worthwhile endeavor. Often this happens in such a sly way, you hardly realize how destructive it has become.

If you leave things out of place on a regular basis, get in trouble because you let things go too long, and generally put off doing things in a timely manner, do yourself a huge favor. Tune in to the reasons you do these things and how to do what needs to be done when it needs to be done. It will save you (and those who depend on you) a lot of stress.

The Price of Procrastination

An engineering student, Nathan wanted to apply to work with a special robot project in his school. He had known for six months of an application deadline that was coming up on the following Monday.

Sunday evening he sat down at his computer to fill in the application and found that he did not have access to the system due to an unpaid library fee he had overlooked. He also discovered he had to have transcripts sent from his previous college. Because he was tied up with two classes Monday morning, he paid the late fee (with penalties) early Monday afternoon and then was able to get a one-day extension on the application. In the meantime his mom called his previous college and asked them if they could fax his transcript on Tuesday. Ordinarily it took several days to get the request in the system, but she implored their mercy.

An ounce of now is worth a pound of later.

His dad, who had dropped him off at school as usual, was forced to leave work early to take Nathan home to complete the application.

Finally, the task was completed. The next day his transcripts were sent. Nathan (and those he had inconvenienced along the way) had paid a high price of stress and aggravation for what he could have done easily if he had started earlier. Of course he had no way of knowing whether his lateness would count against him as the committee considered his application.

Procrastination has a dark underbelly that is often overlooked but frequently experienced. When we procrastinate, we tend to lose track of exactly where we are in an activity or what we need to do to complete a task. Needed tools and materials get scattered. For example, if we buy ceramic glue to fix a broken piece of pottery and don't do it immediately, chances are the glue will be misplaced. If we decide to replace an electrical switch, buy the switch, but put off installing it, the switch will probably soon be nowhere to be found or we may even forget we bought one. Procrastination made Nathan's job harder than it needed to be. He will not live up to his full potential until his chronic procrastination of little things is conquered.

Dealing with Procrastination

People put things off for a variety of reasons and often these reasons intertwine, working together and strengthening each other.

- Perfectionism is one cause of procrastination and is probably one of the most pernicious because it is based in fear. We don't do something because we are afraid we won't do it well enough or will make a fool of ourselves. Or perhaps we fear we will succeed and have to live with the new circumstances brought about by our success.

- Some procrastinators concentrate too much on emotions. They think they can't accomplish some task unless they are in the right mood. Sometimes they may try to create the right mood. For example, if a job is boring, they create the panic of an immediate deadline to break through the boredom.

- Often circumstances hold up procrastinators. They are waiting for a part to arrive or a price to fall. Maybe they are seriously overcommitted and have no time. Or the environment isn't right (it's too crowded, noisy, or messy).

- Some people have made a habit of riding the wave of adrenaline that comes when they wait until the last minute. They have become expert in knowing just how long they can dawdle before they jump into a project. This may work for simple projects but leaves no room for error and does not work well on complex projects.

Just facing the reason for procrastination does not break its hold. The only way to weaken its grip is by specific actions. Several approaches follow that may help you free the sludge of procrastination from the pipes of your life.

Dull and Boring

Often people put off doing a task that is dull and boring. They may dread doing the filing at work or straightening the living room, so they put off doing the boring job. When this is the case, here are some things to try:

- Make a game out of it. How much can you (and family) do in a given time? (Set a timer and try to finish before it goes off.)
- Mix something fun with the boring job, like listening to an interesting CD.
- Focus on the end result.
- Change your mind-set. Be willing to do boring things. Everything doesn't have to be fun.
- Have a friend work with you. Studies have shown the benefit of working with a partner or just having someone in the room to keep you company. Ask a good friend to sit and talk with you as you sort through the things in your closet. Go to a break room or a teachers' lounge to be with other people while you do paperwork.
- Offer yourself a reward. *When I finish this, I will give myself a root beer float.* (Even if it has to be diet root beer and no-sugar-added ice cream.)
- Delegate or exchange the part you don't like with somebody else.

One puzzling aspect of the I-don't-do-boring attitude is that, once I do a long-delayed task, I often marvel at how easy it was, especially compared with the anxiety and inconvenience of putting it off, and I feel a sense of elation at the results or at simply getting it over with. So why doesn't this memory of tasks turning out to be easy or the anticipation of the elation that comes with completing them motivate me to tackle new tasks?

Big and Uninspiring

There are some jobs that take a long time and offer little reward when we are finished; for example, going through a pile of papers that have accumulated on your desk. You know there are some papers in the mix that need to be saved but many that can be discarded. You dread making decisions about which to keep and then what to do with them.

Set aside fifteen minutes a day and use that time to go through the pile with no thought of filing at this point. Put a sticky note on each paper you decide to keep, telling where you are going to file it. This will keep you from having to read it over again each time you handle it. Give yourself permission to stop for the day when the fifteen minutes is up. Later go back and do fifteen minutes of filing. Doing each part of the job separately is easier and faster than trying to file each paper as you go.

> That which the fool does in the end, the wise man does in the beginning.

Overwhelming and Complex

Some jobs are so overwhelming and complex that we avoid starting them because we're not really sure how to proceed or even if we will be able to do them. For example, you may want to add a room to your house or set up a website, but the job seems overwhelming. You may have decided to write a book or start a business, but taking the first steps is intimidating.

To get started on a complex job, try the following:

- Clarify your goals and the process it will take to accomplish them.
- Prioritize the steps of the project.
- Use mind mapping or create a time line for accomplishing specific steps (see chapter 10).

- Try to break the job into parts and focus on one part at a time.
- If you are having trouble clarifying your goals, ask someone to listen to you talk through your idea or plan. Just being able to talk it through often helps.
- Do something. Gather preliminary information; get phone numbers; write down relevant thoughts; list the names of others involved. Taking a small step will help you get involved in the project.
- Break the job into baby steps. Rather than washing all of the windows in the house, just wash the windows of one room. Or wash just one window.

Stuck at a Certain Point

Sometimes we get to a certain point in a task or activity and can't seem to go any farther. For example, if you are knitting a sweater and can't follow the pattern's explanation of how to put in the sleeves, the project may go unfinished. Or you may start cleaning the basement but there are so many old items you don't know what to do with, you get discouraged and stop in the middle of the job.

- Ask a friend for help so you can move on.
- Tell yourself you'll do just a small part of a job that seems too big.
- Schedule time each week to work on the project until it's done.

Not Important Enough

As life goes on, our priorities change. The task that seemed so important at one time may lose its importance if it is not done right away. For example, you may have planned to upgrade the basement so the kids could use it as a playroom.

But the kids have grown older and don't need a playroom anymore. At one time it seemed important but now it doesn't. Reevaluate to decide if redoing the basement is really where you should spend your time. If it is, take the first step to begin. If it isn't, make a conscious decision to discard the plan, so you can turn your attention to other more important things without feeling guilty.

Small Annoyances

There are jobs we know we should do, but we procrastinate because we can get by without doing them, even though they can be annoying. For example, your front door lock is cranky. Rather than getting it fixed, you struggle with it on a daily basis. It takes only a second to pry the door open with a screwdriver you keep on hand, and you forget about the problem as soon as you get inside.

Small undone projects like this never get on the to-do list. It may be the scratch on the dining room chair you should refinish, a broken zipper that keeps you from wearing a favorite skirt, or the phone numbers in your speed dial that need updating. Most of these would take only a few minutes to fix or to arrange to have fixed but you can live with the slight inconvenience they cause, so you do. It always seems more important to do something else.

The problem is that enough of these small annoyances can cut into the quality of your life.

Make a list called: "Bothersome, Nonessential To-Do Items" to remind yourself to take care of each small job. Write these things down to keep them in focus so you won't forget to do them. Tell someone about how you are going to fix the problem. Often these jobs can be delegated or done at odd moments.

Difficult to Start

Often a job is put off because there are steps you will need to take before you can actually get to the job. You may have trouble accessing the materials, tools, or information that are needed, so you procrastinate.

For example, you may need to fix a screw that is coming loose in a fan. It's a small job, but you need the toolbox that is stored on a top shelf in the shed. You will need to use a stepladder to reach it and it is very hot (or cold) out in the shed. So each time you think of fixing the fan, you remember how difficult it will be to get the toolbox, and you put it off again.

Or you may need to make a call to a certain handyman whose card you have kept. You know it is "around here someplace." You will look for it later when you have more time (and patience).

To prevent being sabotaged by not having easy access to the things you need, organize your household items for easy access. If what you need for a project is available, you are much more likely to do it.

Not Enough Immediate Reward

It is often the long-range tasks that don't have immediate rewards that are difficult to begin and stick to until they are finished. For example, you may want to go back to college, but it will be a long time before you graduate.

Here are some things to help you keep going when you have to wait for the rewards of completing a project.

- Visualize the end result. If possible, post a picture that illustrates what you are working toward. (Remember the guy who has a bulletin board of goals, including a picture of a college he wants to have named for himself?)

- Change your perspective. Remind yourself that time passes quickly. If you don't do the work, you won't have anything to show at the end of the extended time. If you do the work now, you will have a good result later.
- Give yourself interim rewards at designated intervals in your work.
- Create a timetable so you can know you are on track and can see progress. It will look like a series of short-range tasks.
- Make lists of what you need to do, so you can cross things off and see your progress.

Major Snags

Sometimes in the middle of a project, there is a major problem that we don't know how to solve and it keeps us from continuing. Examples might be: you can't get your new computer program to perform; the books you need for your research are not available at the library; the cabinets you bought for the kitchen don't fit in the space available to them.

Here are some things to try:

- Talk to somebody who has prior experience in the area.
- Get together with others and brainstorm about a solution.
- Take a break. Change your scenery. Walk around. Get a snack.
- Call in an expert in the field of your problem.
- Give it a little time to see if it will begin to solve itself.
- Try a new process or idea. Will any other approach accomplish your goal?
- Keep it simple. Get back to basics and see if the problem is there. For example, if your computer doesn't work, check to see if it is plugged in.

Distasteful and Emotionally Unpleasant

There are some jobs or activities we put off because we know they will be unpleasant, for example, going to the dentist or resolving a serious error you made at work. To tackle such tasks, we must learn to focus on what we will achieve, not on the job itself. Don't think about the details of the dental appointment. Concentrate on the benefit after your visit. Don't think about the job to be done. Focus on the result.

Some things require all of the strengths of maturity. The difficult jobs require character and responsibility. They also benefit from prayer. Pray for peace before the visit to the dentist and wisdom in how to resolve the error.

The serenity prayer asks for "courage to change the things I can." It also reminds us that we need to accept the things we cannot change. It is not procrastinating to accept that there are some things we cannot do.

Chronically Putting Off a Specific Job

For some reason, unknown to you, putting off one reasonably simple but necessary task is becoming a habit, and each day increases the importance for getting it done.

Psychologist Albert Ellis suggests you set a time deadline and punish yourself if you don't do the task by that specified time. Vow not to watch TV or even to eat until the job is done.

Another very effective method is to sneak up on something you have been putting off by doing one little part of the job to break the ice.

- If you need to clean the oven but you don't want to, gather the cleaning supplies and place them near the oven. Sticky note a date on the supplies and put them away if you haven't done the deed by then.

- If you need to update your Christmas card list, put last year's list in a chair you sit in regularly. (Caution: Be careful not to leave those items you use as prompts sitting out for such an extended time that they become clutter.)
- If you need to rearrange the utility room (barn, shed, basement, and so on), open the door and draw a schematic of how you think it should be done and make a list of any new supplies you need to buy. Tape the schematic to the door. Write a target date for completion. This is a beginning. You have broken the ice and may just find it easier to actually finish the job later.

Sick or Chronically Tired

Some low-grade sicknesses masquerade as fatigue from overwork or lack of rest. If you always feel tired, even though getting enough sleep, ask a doctor to check whether your iron is low or your thyroid is not functioning properly or you have some other condition; such as depression, that saps your energy. Persevere until you find the help you need; then follow the doctor's advice.

Finishing the Big, Ugly Task

Jane and Roberta were office staff buddies in a small plant that made tubular furniture in northern Indiana. They made a great team. They worked in the same large cubicle and shared job responsibilities. They were both detail oriented and reliable. The boss knew he could count on them to do a good job on any project he assigned them.

Because they were capable, the boss dumped on them an important project nobody else wanted. It was tedious, complex, demanding, unpleasant, and boring. It was very long-range but it was crucial for the future of the firm.

As Jane and Roberta dove into the project, they outlined the steps they could foresee. Since it was a long-range program, they set small rewards at certain points to keep themselves motivated and enthusiastic. To overcome tedium, they made a game out of it whenever they could and told themselves it was fun. They would give each other challenges, such as, "I'll bet you a soda I can get this information from shipping by noon."

When they got stuck, they had a few tricks up their sleeves to move themselves forward. They would take an M&M break, go for a walk and brainstorm, or call on a fellow worker who had some experience in the sticky area.

Working together made the project bearable. They were accountable to one another and leaned on each other for moral support. Moving forward at a steady pace, they finally finished the project. They would say the secret to their success was that they never let tasks sit on their plate for very long.

Because of their performance, their careers were rewarded.

Quickie Tips for Overcoming Procrastination

- Write a specific time for completing a task in your planner. A specific time gives you more determination to do a job. Set your computer to keep bringing up a reminder.
- Start with doing a part of the job you enjoy. Any part you do will be a beginning.
- Tell someone else (like a friend, a colleague, or someone in an accountability group, such as those on www.messies.com) what you are going to accomplish.
- Talk out loud to the job. Aggressively challenge your feelings and face the job itself by verbalizing how you feel and how you are going to get the job done.

- Get rid of clutter that stands in the way. It may be what is holding you up.
- Get started now, especially if it's a small task. Abide by the thirty-second rule: If it takes thirty seconds or less, do it immediately.

  It's amazing what can be done in thirty seconds. You can file a paper or two, take items to the bedroom that belong there, or hang up the coat you just took off.
- Set a timer and give yourself permission to stop working on the task after ten minutes, a half hour, or any specific time. See how fast you can go and how much you can get done.
- Practice productive procrastination—when you have one job you can't make yourself do, shift over to another job. It is better to have another useful task waiting in the wings than to go to some totally nonproductive task, such as playing a computer game, watching TV, or talking on the phone.
- Do a little at a time; nibble it to death. Do five minutes a day and watch the job dwindle. A pile of papers to be filed, clothes to be folded, or emails to be handled cannot withstand the assault of repeated little attacks.
- Do it carelessly. If perfectionism is holding you back, just do it, maybe even in a deliberately slipshod way to break the hold perfectionism has on you.
- Strike when you are on a roll. One day when you feel good, the weather is pleasant, the moon is in the second house (or whatever), and you have time, jump in and do what you have been putting off.
- Delegate some or all of the job. Maybe this particular job is not your thing right now, so ask someone else to do it.

- Act as if. Become an actor and pretend you are an achiever who can and will do the task that awaits you.
- Gather your tools together. This may move you to actually doing the job. Set a time to put the tools away. Do the job before your designated time for quitting.
- Concentrate on changing your habit. If you chronically leave something undone, force yourself to do that one thing regularly. Realize you don't need to like it to do it. At first, it will irk you. Later it will become automatic and easy.
- Reward yourself. When you complete a project, give yourself a reward, something special you won't give yourself until the job is finished—maybe lunch out with a friend, a piece of jewelry, or something for the house.

> God, grant me the serenity to accept the things I
>   cannot change,
> Courage to change the things I can,
> And the wisdom to know the difference.

The next chapter will help you break through roadblocks by suggesting a variety of specific, easy-to-do techniques.

Your Turn

☐ Name three areas in your daily life in which you chronically procrastinate. Why do you procrastinate here? Choose a plan of attack.

1. _____

   Why? _____

   Plan: _____

2. _____

   Why? _____

   Plan: _____

3. _____

   Why? _____

   Plan: _____

☐ Name three long-term goals you are procrastinating about.
   Why? Choose a plan of attack.

   1. _____

      Why? _____

      Plan: _____

   2. _____

      Why? _____

      Plan: _____

   3. _____

      Why? _____

      Plan: _____

☐ Name three short-term goals you are procrastinating about.
   Why? Choose a plan of attack.

1. _____

   Why? _____

   Plan: _____

2. _____

   Why? _____

   Plan: _____

3. _____

   Why? _____

   Plan: _____

Choose a time to get these done. Write down the area and time target in a place you can see them often, perhaps in your daily planner or on a list that's close by your computer.

Tips

1. You know your real deadline. Now give yourself an earlier false deadline so you will be finished early. Include the artificial deadline in your computerized or paper planner.
2. Write it down. Give yourself a definite time to get the job done.
3. Start with a part of the project you enjoy.
4. Make a commitment about your project to someone else. Be accountable to them.
5. Set a timer and commit yourself to start working for a certain period of time even if it is short. You will

have broken the ice and completing the job may seem easier.

6. Use the slogan, Just do it! Try not to base your starting on whether or not you feel like it.

True or false?

1. I don't like to write out the steps of a project; I usually wing it.
2. I sometimes skip doing activities because they are difficult to organize.
3. I don't use a day planner. I just remember or make notes on paper.

Answering true to any of the above makes you a good candidate for the information in the next chapter. You will love the useful and fun methods given below that will make organizing of projects easy.

---

10 easy project management

getting started

The nicest thing about not planning is that failure comes as a complete surprise, rather than being preceded by a period of worry and depression.

Sir John Harvey Jones (tongue in cheek)

Twenty years from now, you will be more disappointed by the things you didn't do than by the ones you did do. So throw off bowlines. Sail away from the safe harbor. Catch the trade winds in your sails. Explore, dream, discover!

Mark Twain

Almost all of us have projects we are working on, projects that are almost finished but are languishing, and projects that are lurking somewhere in the back of our minds nagging us to get started.

But life happens. Days become filled with trivialities or we get sidetracked from an important project when we run into hindrances or something more exciting comes along. Like Michael, the frustrated middle manager we met earlier in the book, interruptions and meetings kept him from accomplishing his project goals. Perhaps you remember Marshall, the retiree who thought he would write a book, learn Spanish, and plant a vegetable garden. His life had settled into chores and mundane daily activities. He remembered the feeling of pride in business when completing projects was a regular part of his life.

Time Management Choice #4

Take control of your projects.

It is the completing of worthwhile projects that gives our lives substance we can take pride in. We need a system that energizes our projects, evaluates which are the most important, and keeps us moving until they are finished.

Mind Mapping

Our buttoned-down and efficient colleagues use time lines and outlines to plan projects and maybe even computer programs to organize their projects. However, the minds of many freewheeling and creative types become dazed when they try to use the very same techniques that are so useful to their co-workers.

If you are one of the latter types, you will find that mind mapping may open the door to productivity for your kind of thinking. Popularized by a British psychologist, it is a fun and casual approach that clarifies the issues at hand in a nonthreatening way.

Mind mapping is a diagram in which the main idea is written in a central circle and all related supporting ideas are arranged radially around it, sort of like the way a child draws the sun with rays. Onto those beginning rays, other rays are added.

The next time you have a complex project you need to think through and remember to complete, try making a mind map and posting it on your wall to remind you of the parts of the project that need to be done.

While there is an abundance of software available for mind mapping, it's easy to draw your map, using colored pens or pencils. For many, doing it by hand has a creative feel to it.

Here are some guidelines to help you get started:

1. Draw a central circle and write the central topic in it. Then draw lines out from the main circle. As each line is added, label it with one of the main ideas.
2. Lines should be just long enough to label.
3. You can number areas in the diagram to indicate the order in which they need to be done.
4. Don't be perfectionistic about how your mind map looks. Just do it. Some people add little icons, stick figures, and doodles to emphasize points.

Talbot's Mind Mapping Experiment

Talbot's business was his biggest project. He knew its parts but he had trouble envisioning how they fit together. In his business he used three skills, his skill as a consultant, his speaking, and his writing skills.

To clarify his thinking, he drew a circle in the middle of a paper. In the circle he wrote, Talbot, Inc. From that main circle radiated three short rays. At the end of each ray he drew a circle and wrote one of his three skills in each of the circles. From these he drew lines to connect to aspects of his work that were relevant to that area. This simple approach clarified his thinking about how all of these activities fit together and enabled him to evaluate which projects deserved his time and energy.

From this diagram Talbot observed something he had never fully appreciated before. Though writing and speaking did not bring in much money, they were essential supports for his moneymaking consulting. He also realized that he had

Mind Map

to initiate his participation in these two areas, while in the consulting area, clients sought him out. As a result of his observations, Talbot redoubled his efforts in speaking and writing because he realized that, although they did not bring in much revenue, they were essential to his overall success at attracting clients.

Using an Outline

For many people mind mapping works best when they number the steps they need to take directly on the mind map diagram. Then they convert the mind map, already numbered, into an outline.

Patty chose to use this approach to plan a garage sale.

This time she was going to do it right. Two years had passed since her last sale that had been a mess. She had put things out on the lawn, priced a few, and planned to negotiate the prices of each item individually. When several people came up at once asking about prices, she got frustrated and she ended up feeling as though she had given things away.

Now she had regained her resolve and wanted to do it differently. But how? She decided to start with the mind map to help organize her thoughts concerning how to sequence her activities. In the center circle, she wrote Garage Sale and then drew lines out from the circle and labeled them with the different issues she needed to address:

- Signs
- Date
- Prices for the items
- Gather all the items into the garage
- Get friends to help
- Advertise

She felt the first thing she should do was select a date, so she wrote a big Roman numeral one by the "date" line, checked her calendar, and wrote in the date she thought was best on that line.

Roman numeral two was placed beside the "friends" line, reminding her to ask friends to help her. She added short lines adjoining the "friends" line and jotted down a few names. Number three was placed beside the "advertise" line. On lines extending from it, she wrote down several newspapers, along with the reminder to check prices and deadlines. She also listed Craigslist and flyers as possibilities. She continued with the other three main items, listing for each one the activities that would be involved in its completion, without actually performing any of the necessary steps.

Then, mind map in hand, Patty set about translating her map into an outline that was to become her road map to success. The final outline looked like this.

Patty's Outline

I. Select a date
   A. This month?
   B. Next month?
   C. Day of the week?
   D. Saturday
   E. Not the day of Brian's Birthday
II. Friends
   A. Brian
      1. Works on Saturdays
      2. Birthday's coming up
   B. Chet
      1. Phone number
   C. Reggie
      1. Too critical. Last choice
      2. Good helper, though
   D. Melanie
      1. Great choice; I hope she's available!
III. Advertising
   A. Newspaper
      1. Dan's brother works for the Herald
      2. Find out if free advertising is available
   B. Local Publications
      1. Get prices. Maybe it's free?
   C. Store Bulletin Boards
      1. Grocery store
      2. Hardware store
      3. Megan's school
   D. Flyers
      1. Post on light poles
      2. Hand out at street corner
      3. Megan's school

IV. Items for Sale
    A. Gather from around the house
    B. Gather from storage unit
    C. Gather from attic

V. Pricing
    A. Don't forget to price everything before sale date
    B. Remember to start this ASAP
    C. Items without prices cannot be in the sale

VI. Signs
    A. Make cute signs
        1. See if the art class will help
    B. Signs are important to buyers

Step-by-step, as she got ready for the sale, she checked off each task until she had covered all of the steps. On the day of the garage sale, her friends came over early and set out the items she had already priced.

At the end of the day she had made $792 and sold everything except an old dress missing buttons and a shoe with a broken heel. These she happily threw away. She counted the garage sale a success and took her helpful friends out to dinner.

Using a Day Planner

A day planner is simply a calendar in which each day is broken into the time segments of a day. The person using the day planner lists for each day what needs to be done, assigned to a specific time, so that tasks are accomplished in a timely manner. When a day planner is used and followed, a project stays on track and moves forward smoothly because each step has been thoughtfully planned and recorded.

You may wish to use any one of the many paper and computer-based day planners. Remember, their chief strength is that you choose specific times for each step.

Most creative and productive people have several open projects going at once. To keep them all moving to completion, a well-thought-out system is needed. That is the purpose of the next chapter.

Your Turn

☐ Clarify one of your complex projects by mind mapping it. Follow the steps below:

Draw a circle. Put your project's name in the circle.

Draw three or more lines out from the circle.

Write your main responsibilities in the project on these lines.

Draw branches off of each line and write on the branches tasks to complete.

Continue expanding your mind map with important tasks and points to remember.

Now that you have an overview, you can address each area individually.

☐ If you desire, make an outline of your project and put the steps in your day planner.

Tips

1. To make it crystal clear to yourself, write out the desired outcome for your project.
2. Set boundaries by writing the points you want to cover. Mention what you won't cover.
3. Stay focused by writing the main goal of your project on a three-by-five-inch card and posting it in a prominent

place or set a spot on the computer or PDA that brings it to the fore.

4. The phases of a project are defining, planning, execution, and completion. It will clarify your thinking if you keep in mind the phase of the project you are in.
5. Before you start, plan a celebration that will mark the end of each project. Stop and smell the roses.

Yes or no?

1. Do important projects sometimes grow cold and uninteresting before you finish them?
2. Are you sometimes surprised to come across a good idea you had forgotten?
3. Do you find yourself working on the projects that are easy rather than the ones that are important?

If you answered yes to any of the questions above, you will really profit from the method suggested in the next chapter. Try it and watch your productivity soar. Managing projects is an art form that you can learn.

---

11 working with your projects

the project notebook

The secret of success is constancy to purpose.

Benjamin Disraeli

I never could have done what I have done without the habits of punctuality, order, and diligence, without the determination to concentrate myself on one subject at a time.

Charles Dickens

Very few projects are simple. Even those that appear to be so, often are not. For example, it seems as though writing a book is just a matter of sitting down and typing until all of the pages are filled. However, in addition to complex research required for some books, organizing and developing the plots and themes of fiction, and the chapter progression of nonfiction makes such a project more complicated.

UPS (Uncompleted Project Syndrome)

Most projects are complex by their very nature, requiring the working together of many varied parts. Even if they seem simple when we first begin them, Murphy's Law comes into play and projects become unwieldy. We have already seen how mind mapping is designed to bring clarity to a multifaceted and involved endeavor. Other methods such as time lines and outlines are useful as well in defining and organizing what we want to do.

If one project is complex, having several projects to do all at once can become chaotic. Planning, executing, and completing a single project is one thing, but keeping several projects going well enough to finish them is a very different proposition. It is common for creative people to begin one project and, in the midst of trying to finish it, happily dash off to another, leaving the first one in limbo. Whether it is half-done craft projects, home improvement tasks, or new ideas for an enthusiastic entrepreneur's business, uncompleted projects lie in the wake of these creative and distractible folks.

Brad's Problem

Brad, a creative type who thrived on new ideas, was drowning in projects. Uncompleted undertakings defined his life. For every project he finally brought to completion, six more remained incomplete. They got cold and he lost interest after a while. No matter how he tried, he could not seem to get them over the finish line. He admitted to himself that he is a flawed perfectionistic procrastinator. He berated himself mercilessly, thinking that he might shame himself into action. But nothing worked. Often he pulled up short with the job 95 percent done. He knew his business would not, could not, thrive unless he overcame this roadblock in his behavior.

Like Brad, most people who struggle with multiple projects do so because they are not completing in an orderly fashion the ones they have started. People who quickly knock out jobs they start are not faced with an overwhelming backlog of unfinished work.

Brad's Solution

Out of frustration Brad decided he had to do something. He made a list in random order of all the projects he had started but never finished, just as they occurred to him. There were lots of them. Some were jewels that had been deserted in mid-production. Then he went through and picked out the most important ones, putting an A beside each of these. He found he had five priority projects.

To preserve his commitment to these five important jobs, he created an individual page in a three-ring binder for each one, and thus developed a project notebook. Now he did not have to remember what his projects were. With a great sense of relief, he realized that the whole group was listed in black and white on his master list and that the five most important were within easy access on the five pages dedicated to them when he wanted to work on them.

A similar list can be made on a computer, with the advantage of being able to be color coded and typed in various fonts to highlight the most important projects on the list. For some, a manila project folder will do as well or better than a project notebook.

Turning his attention to his first A project, Brad began filling out his project page, listing the steps he needed to take. This project was "Complete website." To further keep his attention focused until the job was done, he taped at eye level above his desk a three-by-five-inch card with the words "Finish Website" written on it. Anytime he was tempted to drift away to some other project, the card helped bring him back to the task at hand.

Brad had created a five-page website. By mistake he had had his webmaster post it on the Internet with two unwanted pages included at the end. These pages needed to be removed. His first step was to contact his webmaster. He also needed to contact three companies to link to their sites as affiliates. Then he had his webmaster put on the links.

The project was less complicated than he had envisioned it would be. So step-by-step he did what he needed to do to cross off each task. And then the project was done! He removed the reminder card from above his desk. He was out from under the burden of the nagging feeling that he should be doing what he was neglecting. Now all he needed was to direct traffic to his site. But that is another project.

Encouraged, Brad went back to his project notebook and filled out a title for each of his other A projects. He selected one and wrote the reminder card for above his desk. Then he turned his attention to finding B projects and filling out the title on each page for those. The C projects stayed on the master list until they moved up to a higher level, were delegated, or became unimportant and never got done.

Project Notebook Instructions
Steps to Planning Your Project

1. List all of your projects on the master projects list and put them in a 3-ring binder
2. Assign each project on your list a priority (A, B, C)
3. Give each "A" project a project sheet and put it behind a page divider with the name of the project
4. Give each "B" project a project sheet and put in the section behind the dividers.
5. Put the project name on the top of each sheet and complete the sheet for each project.
6. "C" projects stay on the list until they are either crossed out or moved up to a higher priority.

To-Do's

7. List all of your to-do's on the To-Do list. To-Do's are simply one-step projects, and don't need a project sheet. (Or put in a section for "A" Projects.)

Project Master List

Date Listed	Project Name	Priority A B C	Note

To-Do List

Date Listed	Project Name	Priority A B C	Note

Project Sheet

Project Name: _____   Priority **A   B   C**

1. Today's Date _____   Estimated Project Completion Date: _____
2. Describe the Project (Purpose and/or Goals)

   ☐ Revisions needed?
3. Gather information. What information are you missing in order to get started?

4. Decide how you will break your project into doable steps. (Will you use a:

   ☐ Timeline ☐ Spreadsheet ☐ Outline ☐ List ☐ Mind Map or ☐ Other?)

5. Gather Supplies: (What supplies do you need to buy and/or have available in order to get started?)

6. List the steps to completion   Should be completed by:

☐		
☐		
☐		
☐		
☐		
☐		
☐		
☐		
☐		
☐		
☐		
☐		

7. Notes or revisions to the project

8. Project Completed!

In addition to the pages in your project notebook that are concerned with each project, you will want to add a page for your master to-do list, which will be dealt with in the next chapter.

Your Turn

☐ Set up a project notebook or computer folder with the kinds of pages shown and begin using it ASAP.

Tips

1. Create a time line for your projects so you will know the steps and timing of each one.
2. If your project gets off track, stop and readjust your time line before continuing.
3. Try creating a flow chart for your project.
4. Break overwhelming tasks into small steps.
5. Enjoy the process as well as the outcome.

True or false?

1. I keep a running list of what I need to do on the back of envelopes or on scraps of paper.
2. I do what I remember to do. If I forget something, probably it wasn't very important.
3. I want to be spontaneous, to do things on the spur of the moment.

If you answered true to any of these, that's a great big "uh-oh!" You need a method that will help you handle activities in a way that works consistently well. Read on.

---

12 to-do list

*keep on top
of your important activities*

Our most valuable asset is time, and successful achievers
spend this precious commodity more carefully than money.

Zig Ziglar

Terrie is eighty years old and needs a knee replacement but
refuses to get one or to slow down. She has raised nine children and now is caretaker for one son who was badly injured
in a car accident. She volunteers to do washing and mending
in a religious retreat house, coming in at seven and leaving
at about one o'clock a couple of days a week. She runs a be-
reavement group as well. In the summer she teaches lapidary
science in the mountains of another state. She loves to keep
busy helping others and makes sure she does not sit around.

Her busy and creative life is full of tasks. When asked how
she organizes her busy schedule, her immediate answer is, "Oh,
I don't organize at all; I just let things pop up!" She throws up
both hands to illustrate the popping. With a twinkle in her Irish
eyes she adds, "I told my family I don't ever want to grow up."

But don't get the wrong idea about Terrie's schedule. She
is unwittingly misleading us. Like so many organized people,
she organizes herself so automatically and easily that she

hardly recognizes that she has a system to her many activities. When pressed, she does seem to recall a few things she does to keep her schedule in line.

"Well," she says as though it has just occurred to her, "I do make a list at night before I go to bed of what I have to do the next day. If I wait to make a plan in the morning, my thoughts might get blown away with the breeze during the night."

Then the woman who doesn't "organize at all" tells that she divides her list of things to do into four quadrants on a piece of typing paper. The first quadrant holds her priority activities, the second is a list of things she needs to do for others, the third is appointments, and the last lists optional activities that may or may not be included in her day's schedule.

In addition to listing them in four quadrants she groups them by priority with the most important first in the list and the least important last. She also groups them by location, putting all of the car errands together and so on. Then she checks them off as she accomplishes each item on the list.

She adds that just after her husband died, she had so much to do that she had to stop listing things on her to-do list because it made her nervous to see how many there were. Thinking about it kept her awake. When her life righted itself somewhat after that loss, she returned to making her list.

Handling Everyday Stuff

Our lives, like Terrie's, are full of a lot of simple but very important activities. They are not part of our overall life goals nor could they be said to be projects. They are, however, essential parts of the fabric of our life and they move us happily forward in what we want to accomplish. Avoid trying to remember them each day or writing them on the back of an old envelope. They belong on a to-do page.

More complex projects are best kept separate on your project list that is kept, hopefully, in your project notebook or computer folder, not on the to-do list. Less complicated activities, on the other hand, are kept in one of the quadrants on the to-do list. (Don't confuse these with the priority quadrants made popular by Stephen Covey, which we discussed in chapter 5.) Your to-do list in the form of quadrants is a list of daily activities you refer to each day.

> Today is a gift. That's why it is called the present. Open it carefully, use it wisely, and don't forget to say thank you.

First you fold a piece of standard notebook-size paper into four quadrants (like Terrie does) and mark them off with a pen or marker. Write the date in the upper right-hand corner.

Label each quadrant with the type of list it contains. Terrie used Priorities, Helping Others, Appointments, and Optional. We suggest using Do, Write, Call, and Buy. Most people find these headings work well for categorizing the tasks they need to accomplish, but feel free to adjust the labels to meet your needs.

- Under Do, you would write things like, "Move items into new purse," and "Set up conference room for meeting." If you like to draw, sketch a picture of a house or the office by the word Do.

- Under Write (which includes anything you do on the computer or write on paper), you might have, "Check out www.messies.com website" (this is a hint) and "Order time management book." Your picture here might be of a little computer.

- Under Call, note any calls you need to initiate or return. For many people, this is often the most crowded part of the list. You may even need to give it more room than its quadrant allows by crowding into a less used quadrant. Of course the picture here could be a telephone.

- Under Buy, include anything done in the car, such as returning something, looking at something ("Investigate possible storage unit at _____"), or buying something. "Purchase gift card for Buddy" goes here as well. Because it covers several kinds of activities, some people call this quadrant On the Go. You may want the picture of a little car zooming around.

Once you determine what divisions work best for you and you have made the quadrants the right size with proper headings and pictures, make several copies of the page and have blank copies ready for use as one fills up. Punch holes in the pages and keep the fresh sheets in the back of your notebook. Clamp the current page on the front of the notebook.

Using Your To-Do List

Since you will be writing your to-do list as things occur to you, the items will not be in priority order. Some people put a red dot beside the most important things to be done. Others draw a double asterisk (**) beside the most important and a single asterisk (*) beside the next. Still others use the letter A for priorities and go down the alphabet from there. Indicate in some way which task is the most important.

You may have as many as fifteen items in each quadrant, though some people like to limit the number to six or fewer. Put a little box to be checked beside each activity you schedule. That is better than crossing it off as you do it. The empty box creates a point of tension—it is not happy until it is filled with a checkmark.

Be sure to write enough information so you know what you meant when you come back to your list. You may have written, "Contact Karina about books," but when you come back to the list, you can't remember who Karina is or what you wanted to do with those unknown books. Instead put, "Call Karina Smith about selling books on eBay," and add her phone number. When the page gets pretty full, write the jobs that remain undone on a fresh page. Each page can represent one day or one week, depending on how active your life is. If desired, you can archive the used and dated pages when you move on to a new page. You may want to keep the old pages because some information may be useful in the future.

You need to drop the one or two low-priority (or no-priority) activities that just keep being transferred from list to list without ever being done (unless you think that sometime in the near future you will actually get to them). These are tasks that may have seemed important at one time but not anymore. Perhaps somebody else nudged them on your list. Now you can't afford it, or you have lost interest. If you want to remember to do them some day in the distant future, transfer them to a long-term master to-do list that we discuss below.

Keep your list within easy view and reach, perhaps clamped to the front of your day planner, your project notebook, or a special notebook that holds this latest list in addition to back lists you have kept for reference.

A to-do list you keep on your computer will not need to be discarded because the done jobs can either be deleted, moved into another area (if you want to keep track of the fact that they are done), or designated as done by changing color or font. If you use one of the programs that probably is already on your computer, make it readily accessible with one click if it is not on default to appear on your desktop.

To-Don't List

Perhaps seeing how many tasks are on your to-do list has awakened you to the fact that you have got to pull back from some perfectly good activities because you simply don't have the time. Make a note of the things that can be eliminated from your responsibility, obligation, or interest. Maybe they are good and you love them, but they are not good for you at this time. If possible, pass the responsibilities to someone else.

"Do what you do, do well," goes an old song. The application of that means you should not spread yourself too thin.

> Your level of success in life is directly proportionate to your level of planning for it.

The Master To-Do List

As you know, to-do items are short little tasks that need to be done. They are one- or two-step activities that are less complex than projects. They can be listed on the quadrant sheet. However, you may need to remember other important things that do not need to be done immediately. As you think of them, jot down on a master to-do list anything you think you want or need to do in the future. For instance, you may want to remember to ask Verbina about when the fruitcake sale is this holiday. Write it down and include Verbina's phone number. Since the sale is several months away, the phone call can wait. You just don't want to miss the sale, so write it on your master list.

Then each time you fill out a quadrant sheet, look at your master to-do list and transfer tasks that need to be moved to the current list.

Stars of the Show

If you use only two tools from this book (that would be unfortunate), make them the to-do list and a calendar. Get started using a to-do list right away. You will get hooked on it, because it will free your mind from trying to remember everything you need to do and it will fuel your energy. Thus you will be freed up psychologically to attend to the important things and focus on the important, complex activities of your day.

Not every activity that needs to be done should go on your to-do list. Some should be delegated to others and put on *their* to-do lists as discussed in the next chapter.

Your Turn

☐ Begin immediately by making your four-quadrant to-do list. Find a place where it can be easily accessed for use all day long. Get a notebook to store back lists or begin using the program in your computer.

☐ Punch holes in the to-do lists and put them in your notebook.

Tips

1. Create a master to-do list.
2. Create a daily or weekly to-do list.
3. Set aside fifteen minutes a day to do the things on your daily list. You'll be surprised at what you can get done in only fifteen minutes, and once you get started, you may even want to continue.
4. Group your to-do list by activity types.
5. Prioritize the activities and do the important ones first.

True or false?

1. I like passing on jobs and training others to do them.
2. I am comfortable with delegating authority.
3. I need more help to meet my responsibilities.

If you answered true to any or all of the above, you will enjoy the next chapter. If you answered false to any, you still need the chapter, because delegating does not just involve your needs; it is a team concept.

---

13 delegate

build a team

Never tell people how to do things. Tell them what to do, and they will surprise you with their ingenuity.

General George Patton

Life is complex. We all have multiple responsibilities, some simple and some complicated. Not many of us can carry the whole load ourselves. Nor should we. Even the Lone Ranger had Tonto. Failure to delegate appropriately will wear you out and will stifle the progress of what you want to do. Effective delegation is one of the big keys to success whether it is in your home or business. Delegation pays off because it releases your time responsibilities so you can do things more appropriate to your abilities, things others can't do. At the same time, by mentoring others, you are helping them build their skills.

Delegating Tasks versus Delegating Responsibility

There are two things we can delegate: tasks and responsibilities.

- *Tasks*. Sometimes it is appropriate to maintain ownership of a job and delegate only limited parts to others. In such cases you are usually close at hand to supervise, advise, and train where necessary. These tasks are lower level activities, like filing, running errands, and, in the home, cleaning and fixing dinner.
- *Responsibility*. At other times it is appropriate to delegate responsibility or ownership to someone else and supervise at a distance. These are higher level, decision-making responsibilities, such as doing a business project or organizing a closet.

Obviously, delegated authority carries more weight of responsibility than delegated tasks. If a mom delegates the task of setting the table to one of her children she has trained to do the job, it is not unusual for the mom to retain ownership of the outcome. That is, if the table is not set by the time the food is hot and ready, she feels compelled to quickly do it herself, to get another child to do it, or to scurry around to find the uncooperative child, grousing as she does so. The mom takes ultimate ownership of the job and the child knows it.

However, Mom may take another approach. She may give the job to a child as his or her responsibility and make it clear that the child has ownership and that she has no intention of jumping in and taking back the job if it is not done.

One mom made it plain to her tardy child that the responsibility for setting the table was totally his by gathering the family around an unset table when dinner was ready and beginning slowly to plop mashed potatoes on the bare tabletop. The other wide-eyed kids started yelling for the tardy child to do his job—quickly!

Mom was making a point not only to that child but to the others as well. Setting the table was not a job the child was

Time Management Choice #5

Delegate, delegate, delegate.

doing *for* Mom. Setting the table was *his* job and he owned it. If for some reason he could not do it, it was his responsibility to get somebody else to do it. He had been delegated the authority that goes along with ownership of a responsibility.

Another illustration is that of a sports team. The third baseman is not doing the job of covering third base for the manager because the manager is too busy, too tired, or too unskilled to do it for himself. The third baseman has been delegated by the manager to own that position. How well he does it is his responsibility. The manager evaluates his performance and acts accordingly but he does not run out to third base to take up the slack.

When you take the time and energy to train others to do jobs they can do in your place, you multiply yourself, your accomplishments, and your contributions. You expand your effectiveness even further when you are able to hand over authority for a job you would like to see done but don't have either the time or the knowledge to do. You honor the person to whom you delegate by your confidence. In short, you build a team to "play" in the area in which you are working. If you have done your job well, together you will win.

Why Not Delegate

The assumption is that, if you recognize the need to delegate, all you need to do is learn how. Then you will be on the road to successful delegation. Experience shows, however, this is not the case. There are two reasons managers in business and parents in the home find it hard to pass responsibility to others.

1. *Perfectionist tendencies.* Some successful managers hesitate to let go of jobs for fear they won't be done properly. When the bottom line is affected by how well a job is

done, anxiety makes these managers reluctant to turn over the reins to someone else rather than keep doing it themselves. In short, they lack the confidence that anyone else can do the job as well as they can. In addition, they reason, it will take too much time to train someone else to do the job. They believe it is easier not to delegate. Many moms do not delegate because they want it "done right." They like being needed and find it easier to just do it themselves than to train their children.

2. *Personal concerns.* When groups from business or government talk openly about the problems of delegation, difficult personal issues that usually run under the radar in the office emerge. Often these people express the fear that those to whom they delegate will take advantage of the situation or will use information to gain leverage over them. They fear they will lose the project or they fear someone will sabotage the project to make them look bad. They may even fear job loss if someone else takes all the credit. Unprofessional behaviors that they have seen in action lurk in the background of their minds, making them hesitant to delegate. In this case, they lack confidence in the integrity of those on their team. Parents who derive their self-esteem from the contributions they make to the home may be reluctant to give these up to someone else.

Teaching Soft Skills

Soft skills are personal characteristics, such as friendliness, social graces, a desire to serve. Many find it difficult to delegate these characteristics.

Lynette, a fashion consultant, always looks like she is going to a fashion photo shoot. Clients who follow her advice on improving their image get more promotions, compliments, and dates. They develop a better self-image, and their wardrobes become streamlined. In short, Lynette does an excellent job.

Her huge client base consults regularly with her about small and large decisions concerning their clothing choices and other appearance-related questions. She could easily grow her business if she trained and used other image consultants or if she formed a business liaison with other consultants in her area. But being a perfectionist, she does not want to lose control of any aspect of her business. Her main fear is that her trainees would not have the personal skills that are her strong point.

Lynette is not alone. Like many successful entrepreneurs, she has had no experience with sharing the load of the successful business she has created. She is an excellent consultant, but is she a good manager? From day one, Lynette has done all of the hands-on work herself. Deep down, she may fear that if she trains someone to do her job, that person may learn all of her tricks and become competition. So she procrastinates making a decision to expand, works hard to cover all the bases, and stunts the growth of her company.

If Lynette could break through her reluctance to delegate, she might be surprised at the results she could accomplish.

Managing Team Members

Roy's operation of his architectural firm has always been one of shared team responsibility right from the beginning of a project. Before he offers a deadline for completion of the architectural plans, he asks each team player how much time their aspect of the project will take. Using their responses as a guideline, he writes his proposal. It is a matter of personal pride and professional integrity for Roy to meet his deadlines. His business is known for this.

Somehow Clement, a new associate, was not keeping up with the timetable to which he had committed. What's more, he was leaving work at five o'clock as usual. "We can get an extension," was his solution. This had never been done in Roy's firm, and Roy ended up doing the work himself to get it in on time. Shortly thereafter, Clement had plenty of time on his hands.

> Good supervision is the art of getting average people to do superior work.

The example of Clement shows that delegation does not always work out. Assuming that Clement was qualified to do the job, the breakdown could have occurred in any of five places. In any case, the final authority rests with the person at the top who needs to be sure all five areas are adequately covered.

1. Did Roy set objectives for his people enthusiastically enough?
2. Did he give clear enough instructions? Giving too many details becomes over-management; giving too few is careless management. The key lies in conversation that draws out the plans and understanding of the person to whom the job is delegated to see if he or she is clear on what needs to be done and whether additional training or supervision is needed.
3. Did Roy give deadlines and checkpoints in written form?
4. Did he clarify responsibility and authority?
5. Did he give feedback and follow up often enough and strongly enough?

Perhaps the corporate personality of punctuality was not spotlighted for Clement when he was hired. Or perhaps he was not prepared for some aspects of the job and had to do the work over again, thereby getting behind in his schedule. Maybe if Clement had reported to Roy each Friday, he would have kept on track. It could be that Clement did not realize that his part in the project was such an important aspect of the whole and that other parts waited for the completion of his part. Clearly Clement did not buy into the corporate standards of always getting projects in on time.

This experience proved to be a lesson for Roy. On subsequent projects he made sure that he managed his team members more carefully.

Managing the Home Team

Both business and home management can benefit from using the team model as a guide. In baseball, for instance, the manager needs to make sure the team has the proper equipment, the field is ready for play, and the players know how to play their positions.

At home Mom (or Dad) has the responsibility to train the children early on to do jobs, such as making their beds, cleaning their rooms, and doing their own laundry. In addition to the jobs that relate to their own territory, they need to pitch in with general household tasks like vacuuming, dusting, preparing meals, and cleanup after meals.

Parents delegate for two reasons: they need help in doing all of the household activities, and the children need training for the responsibilities of adulthood. Alert parents keep an eye on the children to determine when they are ready for training. At first, they teach them to do a task by doing it with them and, as time goes by, supervising their actions. Eventually the children do it alone with only occasional supervision to make sure they are not slipping into bad habits.

In the interest of time management, parents should be shifting the responsibilities a little at a time to their children. It is not uncommon for parents to choose to do all or most of the work themselves rather than struggle with resistant children or the effort of training. In the end, this causes problems for both children and parents. Parents do more than they should, and the children are not trained in necessary life skills.

A well-trained child in middle teen years should be able to take over the full responsibility for the whole house for a short time so that if Mom or Dad is away for a week, the household can run just as though he or she were there.

Delegating to Kids

Although Fiona had a busy life with seven children, she did not have a time problem. She expected everybody to do an age-appropriate job each day. She posted the jobs on the refrigerator on a large piece of paper decorated for the season or holiday. Her rule was that only those who had done their jobs could come to the dinner table. Slackers had to do the job before they could join the family.

Because she believed only those who work should get pay, she never gave allowances. Instead she created a money system from altered Monopoly money on which she wrote a job, an age range, and payment. Anyone who wanted money could do the job, have it checked for quality, and receive pay. In that way, extra household jobs could be done.

Your goal is to make your children independent—for both your sake and theirs. Save your time and energy by making it easy for your young trainees to take over activities you are now doing. Here are some suggestions:

- If their beds fit against the wall, pin (with safety pins) the sheets on the wall side of the mattress so the children need to straighten only the outer side.
- If your shower has one handle for regulating temperature, put a waterproof sticker or dot of some kind where the point should aim for the correct temperature. Then the child can bathe independent of your help.

- Lower the bar in your child's closet so he or she can reach it to hang up clothes. Or buy a commercially made attachment to the bar or make your own with a rope and PVC pipe.
- Get rid of deep toy boxes that lure toys into oblivion. Instead, buy shelves or wire drawers so children can access and return toys easily.
- Put a hamper in their room for dirty clothes.
- Draw place setting positions on place mats to show where plates, glasses, and utensils go while the children are learning to set the table.
- At eight years of age, begin training children to do their own laundry (hint: hide bleach during this time).

Changing Hats

Whether at home or work, someone who is used to wearing the workman's hat must move up to wear the management hat if he or she is to ever solve the problem of having too much for one person to do effectively. Making that switch usually comes slowly. But it should come steadily until the delegator has learned the delegating skills well.

When delegating, follow these five steps:

1. Clarify your objective for the person you are delegating to.
2. Give clear instructions, verbally and in writing.
3. Set deadlines and checkpoints so they will know how they are doing.
4. Clarify responsibility and authority so they will know when to check with you and when to work on their own.
5. Give feedback and follow up. Don't hover, but do keep in touch.

Along with learning the delegating skills of this chapter, we need to learn how to handle an area of our lives that can foul up any management plan—interruptions. This is the subject of the next chapter.

Your Turn

☐ Are you a good delegator? To help you decide, answer yes, maybe, or no to the questions below.

1. Would the job you are doing benefit from additional help?
2. Are you comfortable with being in authority and telling others what to do?
3. Are you confident enough about your own position not to fear competition from the one you are training?
4. Do you have good people skills so you can maintain a positive approach among those to whom you delegate?
5. Are you able to hand over the reins for part of a job to another person under your supervision?
6. Do you feel comfortable checking on someone to see how the work is going?
7. Are you able to analyze how the job is organized well enough to know which pieces can be given to someone else?
8. Is growth or improvement an important part of your future goals?
9. Are you a good teacher/trainer/leader?
10. Do you know what to do when the delegation isn't working and are you willing to do it?

- Applaud your yes answers and keep up your good work.
- Work on your maybe answers and try to bring them into the yes category.

- Consider whether you need to receive more training in those areas where you answered no. Read management articles and books or attend seminars on the subject.

Tips

1. Be sure to make your objective clear (post a picture if appropriate).
2. Answer questions and train when necessary.
3. Set a reasonable deadline together with your trainee.
4. Check in from time to time with the person to whom you delegated a job. Give help and answer questions if necessary.
5. Give special attention and encouragement if the job is boring or tedious.
6. Let the person be innovative if it looks like his or her ideas will work.
7. Pitch in if necessary to train further or bring in more help if the job is technical.
8. Praise and thank those who do a good job. If possible, give a bonus or reward.

True or false?

1. I am seldom troubled by interruptions.
2. I have a good system for controlling interruptions.
3. My work and family know my time needs and respect them.

If you answered false to any of these, it means you can benefit from revisiting the problem and finding solutions. When you solve some of the interruption problems, prepare for a big "Hooray!" Keep reading.

---

14 interruptions

regain control of your time

Short as life is, we make it still shorter by the careless waste of time.

Victor Hugo

Things which matter most must never be at the mercy of things which matter least.

Goethe

The problem of interruptions looms huge in the mind of anyone who wants to get things done. Whether at work or home, progress is impeded by constant intrusive obstructions to progress. Usually they are people. Sometimes they are not. That's why we hear so often:

"I could get a lot of teaching done if it weren't for the students."

"The housekeeping would be a cinch if it weren't for the family."

"Business would be better if it weren't for the clients (or the boss)."

"The phone rings incessantly."

People and things can hinder our progress.

Bryan's Two Important Projects

Who would think that on the morning Bryan had come in early to prepare a report for presentation at a ten o'clock meeting, his secretary, Chatty Kathy, would feel compelled to tell him about her son's orthodontic problems? By not being as polite as usual, he was able to shoo her out after a record twenty minutes, as he told her to hold his calls and then closed his door. He also turned off his cell phone and computer. Just as he got immersed in his report, he was dismayed to hear the fire alarm and so he thumped outside wasting another twenty minutes. Back in his office, Bryan had to check some records to calm a disgruntled client who had intimidated Kathy, so she let his call go through. With only an hour left before his meeting, Bryan scurried to put down the information that he needed to present. At the meeting he promised that the edited version would be on the desks of the participants by that afternoon.

> **Time Management Choice #6**
>
> Manage interruptions, distractions, and time wasters.

Working through his lunch hour, he ate a candy bar, typed his report, sent it to Kathy for printing and distribution, and started working on his second project, an important sales projection.

His projection was due at three. On a whim, he quickly dipped into his email and noticed a message from his wife reminding him to pick up the birthday cake for the baby's first birthday party that night. He did not realize how much time it would take to find and mail his wife a cute musical Internet card to make up for his no-call morning.

With his door closed and calls being held, Bryan slipped under the wire with his projection that was very well received. He hung around past closing time for a few minutes to bask in the glow of approval from co-workers.

Though he had sped to get to the bakery before it closed, he had to persuade the owner to open the locked door and let him in to buy the cake. Exhausted and greatly relieved to be through this frenetic day, Bryan arrived home to a happy wife (musical Internet cards do a lot!) and an excited baby. But he dreaded the day's backlog of emails and phone calls he would face the next day, along with his usual hectic schedule.

The day had been a wake-up call for Bryan, one of many wake-up calls he had ignored. But this time he decided to analyze what had gone wrong and what he could do about it. The next day, getting into work early, he wrote his list of what had gone wrong. Interruptions were a big part of the problem, so he listed them.

External interruptions:

- phone calls
- meetings
- visitors
- fire alarm
- family emails
- social obligations with co-workers

Internal interruptions:

- choosing to read email
- choosing to answer email
- choosing to send Internet card

Then Bryan put a check beside what he could have controlled. Clearly he could not have controlled the fire alarm or his boss's meetings. He couldn't have fully controlled Kathy coming into his office but he could have controlled to a certain extent how long she stayed. He had somewhat controlled the phone calls but not completely. He could have ignored his wife's email reminder but he knew that would not have been wise. And even though their praise was heartwarming, he did not have to spend so much time with his co-workers after his presentation. The most unnecessary and time-consuming thing he did was to seek and send the special musical card.

Each of the interruptions, over which he had control, had taken about twenty minutes, adding up to a bite out of his day of more than an hour and a half. Studies show that it takes a staggering twenty-five minutes to refocus fully on a project after an interruption, so not only was the quality of his concentration diminished with each interruption, but it took time for him to get back to really focusing on the task at hand.

After analyzing his day, Bryan realized he had frittered away valuable minutes, and that was not good. He could see further that the real reason he had been behind the eight ball with his two projects was that by not structuring his time on previous days, he had let his work pile up to the last minute. This meant he could not afford to be flexible on the day the projects were due.

In Bryan's case and in many others, the reason the interruptions were so critical is because he had left too much to do in too little time. The long-term solution to interruptions has to do with scheduling, prioritizing, and self-discipline. If Bryan had done part of his work earlier in his week, he would not have experienced the stress that had become his everyday experience.

Creating Balance

The solution to interruptions does not focus primarily on the interruptions. You can't stop them from happening. Some of them are even important. Isolating yourself may waste the time of others who need your input to move ahead with their work, and a certain amount of friendly interaction molds the team together. Also certain bits of "gossip" enable you to keep your finger on the pulse of organizational issues that no other channel will supply you. Wise parents do well to be alert to activities of the household. Though they may come as interruptions, many small bits of information sometimes add up to important insights.

> Live your life so you will never have to say, "If only . . ."

It is a matter of balance. Since you can't stop all interruptions, you need to learn to moderate them to minimize their impact on your goals and plans for the day.

Even the most organized work schedule can be sabotaged by uncontrolled interruptions. Learn to manage them by using a few of the ideas below. Some of them are physical changes that have to do with the room itself. Others are personal habit changes. The personal changes are by far the most difficult to make.

Prevent Interruptions

Think ahead and take the measures necessary to prevent possible interruptions.

- Give your assistant clear guidelines as to what interruptions are appropriate and give him or her the authority to schedule an appointment or send the person to someone else.
- Move your desk so when you are sitting at it, your back is to the door.

- If possible, isolate yourself by closing the door or working in another area, like a conference room, when concentration is important.
- Don't put a welcoming candy dish on your desk and don't store materials that others have to access in your room.
- Commit to blocking off time for priorities early in the morning (or during your best productive time) and "opening up shop" officially only after that hour or hour and a half. At home, reserve the first half hour after the children leave for school to get your priorities arranged for the day. If you have preschool children, use naptime or see if you can arrange for a high schooler to watch them on a regular basis to free up an hour for planning.

Meet Interruptions as They Come

- When someone asks for a few minutes of your time either on the phone or in the office, schedule a time when you can call back or go to that person's office.
- If someone says he or she must talk to you immediately, ask how many minutes are needed or tell the person how much time you have.
- Some people are storytellers and like to give a lot of background for their issues. Help them get to the point by asking them to summarize their need or sum up their point in one sentence.
- Schedule a specific time to help with the request.
- At home, silence your phone and email notification to limit unnecessary interruptions.
- Create a signal or sign so your family members will know when you are working and cannot be interrupted.
- Communicate clearly that just because you are working at home, that does not mean you are free to be interrupted.

Don't Allow Prolonged Interruptions

- Stand up when someone comes in and remain standing to talk. Then the person will be less likely to sit down and will not stay as long.

- Move around in front of your desk and, if the conversation wanders, ask the person to walk with you to the photocopy machine, water fountain (or Coke machine), where you accomplish your errand, talk a little longer, summarize, and leave the person in the hall.

- Remove chairs or put a briefcase or something in the chair to keep people from sitting down.

- Set a time limit and announce when time is up.

- If someone must see you regularly, ask the person to save up several things for one time and bring a list of subjects to discuss.

- Set boundaries for yourself at home so you are clear on when you have work time and when you have free time.

- Communicate this to the family by having a sign that says "genius at work" when you are busy.

- You may want a sign that says "genius is free" when you are available.

Brianna's Personal/Work Balance

Interruptions are the bane of home productivity, as Brianna's story illustrates. On any given day, Brianna has at least a couple of activities to do, some personal, some business. She's busy and active and she likes it that way. A real estate agent in a busy downtown office, often she runs into problems when her personal life and her business life collide.

Since her kids have left the nest, she has been catching up on all the social life she missed earlier as a mom to her three who are now parents themselves. A dedicated, spunky grandma, Brianna makes sure she works her extended family into her life as often as possible.

She loves it that at any time she may hear a little knock on the door from a grandchild who lives close by and wants to share a flower or an invitation to go somewhere. But this easy access does not always work out well for her schedule. Since her family lives so close and her business activities are flexible, the family thinks they can call on her at the last minute to fill in for some responsibility when they were in a pinch.

The whirlwind of her family, social, and business life is wearing Brianna out and interfering with what she needs to do at home. When she tries to get something done, one of her social organizations calls with a lot to say, her business contacts her, some emergency arises, or the kids come over. And there are those undesirable solicitation calls and surveys, to boot.

Somehow when Brianna wasn't looking, too many things got thrown into the hopper of her life; now she has to live with prior commitments and the new ones that keep coming her way to which she keeps saying yes. Something had to be done.

Brianna had set herself up to be interrupted from many sources. It seems that anytime she starts to catch up, someone calls and pulls her away from her activity. She is behind on paying her bills, mail is piling up, the weeds are overtaking her garden, and her laundry hamper is overflowing. Sometimes she picks up takeout for dinner, just because she had not been able to get to the grocery store.

Brianna's solution is obvious and simple but it isn't easy. When she stopped to think about it, she knew what she had to do. Painfully she has begun to say no to new activities and to cut ties with some of her earlier obligations, especially those that had been eating up her time. She loved them all but she just doesn't have room for them in her life at this time. The most difficult task has been to set time boundaries with her family. However, when they set up a schedule of get-togethers, they find that it works even better than the casual haphazard method they had been using.

With fewer interruptions from her friends, family, and many activities, slowly but surely Brianna's books are getting read, her pile of mail has dwindled, bills are paid, her laundry hamper is not overflowing, weeds are pulled, and when she gets take-out food, it is not out of desperation.

Modern Interruptions

Technology, such as cell phones, pagers, landlines, email, instant messaging, texting, and the like open us to interruptions from many sources at any time. Ease of access into our lives is double-edged for both good and bad. In addition to opening lives to distractions, technology enables us to work from home and make important contacts easily.

> Winners make it happen. Losers let it happen.

In an effort to control the problem, anti-interruption technology is catching up somewhat by providing us with voicemail, automatic replies to email, and opt-out opportunities. But the final line of defense against interruptions lies with us.

The Free Wheelers

Some personalities are not comfortable building control into their lives. They prefer living in the moment and taking whatever life sends their way. They say they are open to opportunities. They roll with, and even enjoy, many of the interruptions that come into their lives because they find concentration on one task tedious and boring. They prefer a job or a life with few long-range projects and a lot of variety. This type of approach works for some personalities but it can cut out much that makes life meaningful and productive.

Most will find that their lives become more satisfying as they focus on their goals, set boundaries, and address the fact that handling interruptions wisely works for their good.

Interruptions can waste our time, as do other issues we need to address. The next chapter will help you zero in on some common and not so common things that might be surreptitiously robbing you of your time.

Your Turn

☐ Name unwanted interruptions that hinder your getting your work done. Indicate if they are at home or work. Indicate what adjustment will help control each.

Describe Interruption	Possible Solution
_____	_____
_____	_____
_____	_____
_____	_____
_____	_____
_____	_____
_____	_____

Tips

1. Rearrange your physical space to decrease interruption opportunities, such as moving your desk so you don't face the door.

2. Don't let anything interrupt time you have planned to spend on a project. Consider it an important meeting with yourself.
3. Try scheduling meetings with the people who interrupt you most.
4. Locate a secluded place to work without interruption.
5. Set hours of availability and hours when you are un-available.

True or false?

1. I stay busy but don't feel as though I am accomplishing much.
2. Phone calls and drop-ins interrupt me a lot.
3. I waste a lot of time looking for things.

Obviously, if you answered true to any of the statements, you need to address the problem of how time wasters squander your time. Chapter 15 will help.

---

15 time wasters

take charge

If time be of all things the most precious, wasting time must be the greatest prodigality.

Benjamin Franklin

We cannot waste time. We can only waste ourselves.

George Matthew Adams

Let's suppose you buy a new car of a certain color, and a strange thing happens. As you drive around, you are amazed at how many of that color car you see that you had never noticed before, even though they were there all the time. It is the same with time wasters. They can be all around you but you may not be aware of them until you stop and focus on what is stealing the hours of your day.

On the Job

No matter who you are or what you do, time wasters enter your life every day. Look at the following list and pick out

153

the several you believe are the ones that interfere with your life the most.

- drop-in visitors
- reading unimportant or unnecessary material
- commuting
- email
- waiting (in lines, for someone to call, at traffic lights, and so on)
- inefficient help or help that requires a lot of supervision
- misplaced items
- misplaced papers
- telephone interruptions
- procrastination
- careless work that needs to be redone
- restlessness and too many breaks
- perfectionism
- crisis management
- unproductive meetings
- outside noise
- trying to do high-priority tasks at a nonproductive time of day

Perhaps you have a unique interruption, like having the snack cart park outside your cubicle. With kids around you cannot imagine all of the strange things that "can" and "will" happen to interrupt you.

Think of a time waster that is particular to you.

Dr. Phil McGraw is fond of reminding those who come to him for help, "You can't change what you don't acknowledge." If you have acknowledged several of the time wasters above, you can set about making changes that will help you get important things done in the time allotted.

To further spotlight your situation, ask yourself the cogent question, like one we have asked before, *If things were perfect, what time wasters would disappear from my life?* Then set about making the changes necessary to make them disappear. Any changes you make fall into the categories of physical changes, system changes, and personal changes. Let's look at Franklin as an example.

Physical Changes

Franklin's time waster was having to commute each day to his downtown office. The office had a prestigious downtown address that no longer served its purpose, so he decided to move it to the area in which he lived. Thus he saved the time spent commuting each day. (He saved money as well.) Franklin made another physical change by creating a desktop container to hold papers for his assistant to file. Once made, environmental changes save time without any further input on your part.

System Changes

Franklin's habit was to riffle through daily mail when his assistant brought it to his desk. He loved looking over catalogs and sales brochures, wasting a lot of time. To avoid temptation, he asked his assistant to cull out all but official business mail and the catalogs he specified.

Personal Changes

Personal changes relating to our natural tendencies are the hardest to make. Franklin found that he procrastinated when it came to doing important jobs because they were harder.

Often he chose to spend time on smaller, less significant tasks that were not as important to his business. He decided to pare down his list of priorities, concentrating primarily on the important ones.

In the Home

Because home life is less structured than business, many people find it is more difficult to be organized at home than at work. At home the big time wasters are:

not grouping activities

too much television

excessive time spent on computer games and casual surfing on the Internet

excessive time spent on puzzles like Sudoku or crossword

disorganized habits

failure to schedule or plan ahead

careless delegation

needless phone conversations

unexpected visitors

unnecessary time away from home, shopping, and other activities

overcommitment to nonessentials

looking for things (such as lost shoes, clothes, and missing papers)

Leanne Gets It Together

Leanne stood in her kitchen and looked around at her three children under five years old. She looked at her house and thought about her harried life. "Life has got to be better than this," she said aloud to herself. "Somebody has got to organize this mess." She looked down at the kids and realized it was not going to be them.

Although every day she worked hard going busily from one task to another, when her husband, Dan, came home at the end of the day, he couldn't see what she had done and she didn't seem to remember either. But she was definitely busy. Some days she didn't even have time to make her bed.

What is going on here? she wondered. Weeks would go by when it seemed that she did nothing except take care of the children, which was important, of course, but it was not enough. *Others seem to live fuller lives. I'll make a list of what I do each day*, she decided. *Then at least I'll have some record of my life.*

After breakfast she decided to get down to business with her list. Just as she got out her paper, the doorbell rang. It was the letter carrier who, by mistake, had dropped off a package that belonged to her neighbor. She walked it over to her neighbor's house, kids in tow, accidentally letting the dog out in the process. After catching the dog and visiting a moment with her neighbor, she hurried home to get started on her day. Between helping the kids in the bathroom and refereeing squabbles, she opened her email. She stumbled on a phishing email from a local bank with which she had no account. Being a good citizen, she promptly took time (some spent on hold) to contact the bank to report the fraudulent email. She noticed she had won a prize on Pogo, a game-playing site. So she quickly clicked in to relax by playing for a minute with her online friends.

Looking up, Leanne was surprised to see it was noon, time to feed the kiddies and herself. As soon as she put the kids down for their afternoon nap, the phone rang. It was a friend with a crisis. She was on her way out of town and had promised the pastor she would pick up flyers for him at the print shop. Could Leanne do that for her sometime before tomorrow noon? Reluctantly Leanne agreed. She could fit it in tomorrow morning when she picked up a prescription at the pharmacy. While the kids slept, she decided to fold laundry from the dryer and discovered that the clothes she had forgotten in the washing machine had soured and needed to be rewashed. To rest, she watched TV. On and on it went like that. Her day was not planned. It just happened.

When she listed her activities, Leanne had an aha! moment. "No wonder I don't get anything done," she said.

The next morning, instead of writing what she did as she went along, she decided to be proactive and make a plan. She divided the paper into squares and labeled them Go, Call, Do, and Buy.

In the first square, she wrote the places she had to go, including the pharmacy and the printer. While she was out, she was going to the post office. As an impulse, she added a stop off at the park, so the kids could play. She wrote the names of three people in the Call area. She wanted to finish the laundry and hang a bulletin board she had been promising her daughter she would put up on her bedroom wall, so she wrote these in the Do square. In the Buy category she included shampoo and lipstick that she wanted to pick up while she was at the pharmacy.

The day flowed like magic. Everything on her list was accomplished. Even when unexpected events occurred and drew Leanne off course, she knew to get back to the listed things. Later that evening she even had time to read bedtime stories to the children. Pretty soon Dan was noticing a change, not only in the house but in Leanne as well. The time wasters had started to disappear in the face of proactive planning.

Reflections about Wasting Time

We need recreation or, as the word suggests, re-creation. It may be socializing, doing a puzzle, or taking a walk. Thoughtfully done at the right moment and for the right length of time, these things are not wasteful. Often, however, these activities and others like them are used to avoid doing something more difficult or distasteful but infinitely more important. The day, week, month, or life goes by with important things that would enhance your life and many other lives around you left undone.

A little time wasting day after day may seem unimportant, but unavoidably, it adds up. People don't mind being busy. They do mind being busy and not accomplishing anything significant. A keen enthusiasm for the important things in life will keep us on track. When it comes to how we use our time, we need to do the right thing not the easy thing.

Whether or not you know Longfellow's poem "A Psalm of Life," most of us resonate to some extent with his enthusiastic view that "Life is real! Life is earnest!" Later in the stanzas he states poetically what this chapter has attempted to convey.

> Not enjoyment, and not sorrow,
> Is our destined end or way;
> But to act, that each tomorrow
> Find us farther than today.
>
> Let us, then, be up and doing,
> With a heart for any fate;
> Still achieving, still pursuing,
> Learn to labor and to wait.

One of the things that keeps us doing the right thing is a well-tuned routine, such as you will read about in the next chapter.

Your Turn

☐ As you think about your time use, are there any time wasters that you need to eliminate?

☐ Do you use any device such as a to-do list to keep your priorities uppermost in your thinking? What devices (be specific)?

☐ How would you state the importance of what you do in life?

Tips

1. Leave a time cushion in your schedule to handle unavoidable time wasters. Don't pack your schedule too tightly.
2. Be aware of your top five time wasters and prepare for them in advance.
3. Before beginning a project, be sure you understand the instructions clearly.
4. Avoid perfectionism and procrastination (major time wasters) at all costs.

True or false?

1. Life seems to become jumbled when I have a lot to do.
2. I don't like routine because it is boring.
3. Often I come to the end of the day feeling I haven't accomplished much.

If you feel that any of the statements above relate to many of your days, you will really benefit from the concept of scheduling routine activities in chapter 16.

---

16 scheduling routines

an indispensable tool

A schedule defends from chaos and whim. It is a net for catching days. It is a scaffolding on which a worker can stand and labor with both hands at sections of time. A schedule is a mock-up of reason and order—willed, faked, and so brought into being.

Annie Dillard
The Writing Life

You will never change your life until you change something you do daily. The secret of your success is found in your daily routine.

John C. Maxwell

The concept of routine gets a bum rap from creative people who thrive on variety and dread the boredom of a routine or humdrum life.

Amen to that! It is a terrible thing if important things in life become the same old same old. Life offers too many exciting and important opportunities to let it become simply an unexciting routine. We need to realize, however, that everybody participates in routine activities every day. Regular activities keep us and our families clean, fed, and healthy. The question is not whether we will do them but whether we have a good schedule and will follow it efficiently so we can get to important things that make life enjoyable and profitable. This is what scheduling routines is all about.

Before we go farther, a word of explanation is necessary to those who fear setting up a schedule because it feels rigid and stifling. Scheduling is not an inflexible list that is written in stone. It is a statement of what regular tasks are important to accomplish each day and when you plan to do them during the day. As you become experienced in using and tweaking your schedule, you will find it meets your needs more and more successfully and will become your friend.

Open the Tap

When you create a schedule for routine tasks, you open a tap through which good time management can flow. A schedule is absolutely necessary because

1. It keeps you from forgetting what needs to be done.
2. It protects you from the unsuccessful "What do I feel like doing today?" approach.

Ignore for the moment your A tasks and your A projects that are intermittent. Turn your attention to activities that are part of every day. This chapter deals with these daily activities. After all, this is the stuff that makes up much of life. Once you get the everyday jobs under control, you will be better able to attend to your A priorities.

There are several categories of activities that we need to consider when making a schedule. We need to know the best way to handle the following:

- Routines, such as commuting and answering phones that take up work time; family activities, such as preparing lunches, making beds, doing laundry, loading and unloading the dishwasher, and cleaning.

Time Management Choice #7

Make and use an effective schedule.

- Time-consuming essentials that we don't even think of as tasks, such as sleeping, eating, dressing, and bathing.
- Unexpected interruptions such as a car that overheats on the way to work, a computer printer that won't print, or a washing machine hose that breaks; and crises, such as a sick child who needs to be picked up at school.
- Previous commitments and appointments made in the past.

Eileen's Optimistic Approach

Every day was a new adventure and full of opportunity for Eileen. She woke up hopeful with visions of a happy day. Optimistically she thought the day would take care of itself, so she didn't spend time in the second quadrant mentioned in chapter 5, the quadrant where many life-affirming activities and plans—not urgent but important—take place. While she waited for something good to transpire, life just happened.

Some days it worked out okay, but when something unexpected happened that demanded her attention or time, she was not prepared. Because she had not created a solid approach to time use, she spent many hours in quadrant one, the quadrant for handling emergencies. Often the life she expected to rock happily along hit bumpy spots. Getting the kids off to school and picking them up at two o'clock were the only constants in her day.

Helping with homework, fixing dinner, welcoming her husband, and a little TV at night were the anchors of her afternoon and evening. Only when other people were involved did her life take on some structure because she plugged into their needs.

She had frequent slipups. Her father-in-law was not happy when she didn't pick him up at the airport on time, but he didn't say anything. Later, when they were planning a family get-together and he asked about her daily plans, he was surprised to learn that she had no schedule at all.

He suggested she make a list of things she had to do on a to-do list. She did. With his encouragement she bought a daily planner and started plugging these activities into time slots. This was a big step for Eileen because it had a feeling of commitment she was not quite comfortable with at first.

She planned for a grocery day, laundry every other day, library day (for the children's story hour), and noted when her husband had to work late or was out of town. Her schedule woke her up to what could be done and, because she had carved out usable time, she was able to volunteer to read at the school and to schedule in a weekly Bible class. She even joined a gym and went every other day. Of course, she got off track on a regular basis but, because she had guidelines in her schedule, she could jump back on more easily. Since now she planned ahead, she grouped her chores and did many of them, such as putting dinner in a slow cooker, early in the day. The quality of her life and that of her family increased greatly as she worked her plan.

Home Routine

Part of the daily routine should be spending time planning in the morning. Morning is the best time for planning for most people. In the evening you will have an idea of what needs to be done the next day. Consider your written goals (see chapter 4) and your A activities and tasks (see chapter 12). Make notes to yourself, so you can include them in your schedule. If time gets short, you will know the main projects you need to pursue in the time you have.

Some routine tasks are not done on a daily basis. Writing them on a schedule will make it much more likely they will not be forgotten. Remember the Chinese proverb about the weakest link being stronger than the strongest memory. The fact that you have a previous commitment to yourself in writing will nudge you to do the job you might otherwise avoid doing.

If you have a household cleaning schedule in place, you will be much more likely to maintain your home. You might not actually do every bit of what you have scheduled. However, the fact that you have put something on the list to be done makes it much more likely that at some point you will do it.

Several different methods have been devised for scheduling household chores, some complex and some simple. One that has proven successful is the simple method of choosing to do one general chore a day, such as dust the front of the house, dust the back of the house (or upstairs and downstairs rooms), vacuum front, and so on. (See *Smart Organizing* by Sandra Felton for further explanation.) Even if the whole job is not fully done, doing part will likely suffice. Space chores out as much as seems to work. Throw in an occasional odd job like cleaning the refrigerator, washing the curtains, or replacing the furnace filter.

In addition to doing the tasks you schedule for each day, set a kitchen timer for fifteen minutes morning and evening and, engaging the whole family, give it all you've got for that short period. Concentrate on the top needs like clearing clutter, changing sheets, emptying the dishwasher, and the like. Whatever gives you the most orderly bang for your time-use buck.

People who procrastinate doing regular chores find they can commit to this simple way of doing things and the house shows increasing improvement.

The Flipper Kit of Messies Anonymous (messies.com) offers both a simple and more complex system of household-job scheduling (see *The Messies Manual* by Sandra Felton).

Other sensible approaches will keep you on track. Develop a system that works for you. For instance, use a three-bin laundry hamper, called a laundry sorter, so clothes are presorted when you're ready to do a load of laundry. Most people benefit from doing at least one load of laundry every day to keep it from piling up. Marcia Ramsland, author and professional organizer, suggests that each load be completely done from washing to folding and putting away in the space of the morning to evening of one day. No laundry load should remain in the uncompleted stage overnight. No more unfolded clothes piling up in the basket (or still in the dryer) and no more folded clothes sitting out of the drawer (and sometimes strewn about as a result). What a delightful prospect!

Sidestepping Chronic Problems

Sometimes by working smarter we can circumvent problems. For instance, purses were being stolen while women were in restroom stalls on the Florida Turnpike. When women hung their purses on the hook on the back of the door, thieves reached over the top, lifted the handle of the purse off the hook, dropped the purse and scooped it off the floor as they made their getaway.

Managers put up signs warning of the problem and asking women to be aware but it did not solve the problem. Then they put more security on duty. Still some thieves got through. But when they simply moved the hook to the side wall of the stall, where thieves could not reach, the problem was solved.

When you have a problem, try to solve it in some way that does not involve habit change (being more vigilant) or effort (more security on duty). Sometimes taking time to make a simple physical change solves the problem with little additional effort on your part.

In an office where you don't want visitors to stay for a long time, move the extra chair far away from the desk or put a clock in an obvious place. At home remove the table where everybody drops things as they enter the door.

Some jobs have built-in schedules, such as when high school teachers change classes during the day at the ringing of a bell. Other jobs, such as those of outside salespeople or public relations personnel, require that a schedule be developed. In a corporate structure, the higher the level of authority, the more flexibility is built into the job and the more self-scheduling falls to the individual.

Francine Takes Control

Francine was the secretary to the vice president of marketing at her firm. She was always busy with her regular duties but sometimes, in addition, her hard-working and creative boss would drop into the office on the weekends to do paperwork, reflecting his recent marketing efforts. On Mondays she was greeted with a chair full of papers that represented new things she needed to do for him—papers to proofread and file, reports to type, memos to distribute, letters to be sent, and, well, you get the picture. These things were extras that needed to be done along with her regular duties that included taking calls from sales representatives.

The only way this kind of work can ever get done is to have it prescheduled. Francine had already determined that she would spend a designated amount of time on each type of activity no matter whether it was routine or the result of her boss's weekend flurry. She folded the work she found on Monday into her previously allotted time schedule. She edited for an hour at the beginning of the day when she felt most alert and she quit at the allotted time. She continued to abide by the allotted times for her regularly scheduled jobs, and quit at her usual time. She used her key anchor times—her arrival first thing in the morning, midmorning break, lunch, and afternoon break—as guides for her schedule, fitting her activities around these prescheduled times.

When she first started her job at the firm, Francine had no idea how her work would flow. She would stop what she was working on each time her boss or a co-worker asked her to do something or when a sales representative called. She had no control of her time or activities. In frustration she told her boss she didn't think she was cut out for her job because there were too many interruptions. He told her that her job *was* the interruptions along with her regular office activities. It was her responsibility to figure out how to get it all done.

As a result, Francine analyzed the nature of her activities. Along with her five major responsibilities, she had to handle phone calls from sales representatives about marketing. It was then that she made her schedule and, by tweaking it, came up with a plan that worked.

Francine knew from experience that unscheduled activities ("emergencies") would occur, so she built in a slush fund of time by leaving an overflow period at the end of each block of scheduled time. For instance, if she decided she would dedicate forty minutes to memos, she scheduled an hour, giving herself twenty minutes for interruptions.

She discovered that on most days, as she used this system, most of her work got done. She kept her boss informed about how her production was going in relation to her schedule and in time he began to adjust to her routine.

Let's Hear a Cheer for Scheduling

Scheduling is only logical. If you don't prepare and use a schedule, you end up at the mercy of whatever job shows up at any time. The only way to work a crowded day is to set up a plan for the most important things and do them consistently. A schedule is a deceptively simple, yet powerful tool.

Scheduling your everyday activities may not allow you to get everything done, but it does allow you to get the most important things done. No other approach does.

This chapter deals with a schedule you create to accomplish routine activities specific to your way of life. The next chapter turns our attention to general activities that apply to us all.

Your Turn

☐ If you were to make a schedule of today, what would it look like?

☐ Days vary during the week. Do you have any regular activities you can place in a day planner around which other things will fit?

Tips

1. To make a schedule, be aware of how you are using your time at present. Do these form a pattern?
2. Keep a list of everything you plan to do.
3. Realize some things are fixed commitments and some are flexible commitments.
4. Base your routine on getting the most important things done, not the largest number done.
5. Consistently use the schedule you create.

Yes or no?

1. Does your morning preparation run as smoothly as you would like?
2. Does your evening wind down as smoothly as you would like?
3. Do you feel you accomplish needed daily chores (laundry, dishes, cleanup, and so on) in a timely manner on most days?

If your answer is no to any of these inquiries, read the next chapter with an eye to making specific changes that will improve the quality of your life.

17 daily scheduling

move smoothly through the day

> Have a time and place for everything, and do everything in its time and place, and you will not only accomplish more, but have far more leisure than those who are always hurrying.
>
> Tryon Edwards

Even if you have never written it down, you have a routine for getting off to work, school, or just getting started at home. Everybody does. The question is whether it is a good routine or maybe even the best routine. *Best* is defined here as what will get you the most results with the least effort.

The word *routine* comes from the French word *route*, which means a well-traveled path. Our activities move more quickly when we (and those we live and work with) have clearly in mind a predetermined way to handle ordinary, predictable activities that happen regularly, often daily.

Since life is full of activities, both planned and unexpected, the only way to increase your chance of having a day in which you can accomplish your goals is to have clearly in mind what you need to do, in what order, and at what time.

Morning and Evening Routines

Let's look first at the basic activities that are part of our everyday lives.

A Successful Takeoff

A good takeoff sets the tone of the day.

- *Wake up.* Set a time.
- *Jump up.* Don't lie abed. There's a wonderful world waiting.
- *Make up.* Make the bed immediately, automatically. Don't make it a big deal.
- *Eat up.* Have something nutritious for breakfast.
- *Wash up.* Enjoy a bath or shower.
- *Brush up.* Take care of your teeth.
- *Dress up.* Care for your appearance from head to toe, including hair, shoes, and (for women) makeup.
- *Look up.* Turning your heart upward to God is a good way to start the day.
- *Clean up.* Leave the house in good shape by picking up clutter and caring for the breakfast dishes.
- Add any other tasks you need to do in the morning, like feed the dog or exercise.

A Successful Landing

A smooth landing in the evening ends the day on a positive note.

- *Eat up*. Have a meal planned ahead so you have all the ingredients on hand.
- *Clean up*. This is a family thing; everybody sticks around until the kitchen is completely cleaned up. You may need to involve your family in this slowly.
- *Straighten up*. Have the family do what one children's show calls the ten-minute tidy. Set the timer and all rush around the house tidying for ten (or fifteen) minutes. This will work miracles.
- *Start up*. Take a few minutes to prepare for tomorrow's launch by making tomorrow's to-do list, preparing lunches, putting materials by the door that family members need to take with them, and so on.

Maria's Praise for the Basics of Daily Routine

Maria took the plunge and began using the time and space organizing routine above that she found on the Messies Anonymous website, www.messies.com. She was thrilled and spontaneously wrote to fellow Messies the following message: "The thing that has helped me stay on track is routines. I know it sounds dull and boring, but I have added a few things to my morning and evening routines and voila! I just do them without thinking. I follow Sandra's list: get up, make up the bed, etc. After taking care of myself for a couple of months, I did another important thing: I helped my four-year-old daughter make a list of *her* morning routine. I let her choose pictures and wrote beside it what it was. We hung it inside the closet, and I have her look at it every morning. After we finished the list, my husband said he thought it would be helpful for grownups too. My daughter has had her list for two weeks and hardly refers to it but knows what to do. We're going to make a night routine next.

"We move to our new home in four weeks. I'll do one for my husband then too.

"I never thought I'd have routines or rules like my cleanie mother, but it certainly has helped. I don't panic anymore when people are about to drop by (which is good since our house is on the market). The odd thing is, I have just as much time for sewing as I did when we spent thirty minutes every day looking for lost things!"

Making Your Day Enjoyable

Here are some practical pointers that will help your day go smoothly, give you a sense of accomplishment, and assure that the important things get done.

- *Look over the day's to-do list.* Early on in the day look at your to-do list that you have brought over from the day before. Add anything necessary and identify one or two things that are priorities, things that you must do today.
- *Focus on habit change.* Sometime during the day remind yourself (and those with whom you live) of a habit you are trying to change.
- *Do something nice for yourself.* Do something special for yourself, such as dressing early and well, making a positive connection with a friend, or upgrading the beauty of a spot in your home of office.
- *Take care of yourself.* You are the linchpin that holds your household together or an important part of your office staff, so take good care of yourself. Remember to drink plenty of water, get enough rest, and do not overschedule.
- *Do daily duties.* Choose four or five tasks that you will do each day, such as:

Empty the dishwasher soon after it is finished running.

Wash, dry, fold, and put away a load of clothes.

Plan meals, especially evening meals, in the morning.

In the office, refer to your daily to-do list, check your email, and listen to your phone messages.

- *Maintain inspiration points.* To keep yourself inspired about maintaining your schedule, you need to maintain an inspiration point. Choose one place in your house you keep beautiful and sparkling at all times. Or at work keep your desktop, credenza, or file top clear at all times.

Schedule some activity that, if you do it daily, you feel that you have had a successful day. It may be observing your planning time, reading the Bible or some other inspirational material, putting on makeup, exercising, practicing well one important habit, or something else you can schedule. Doing this can be your inspiration point.

In addition to keeping a regular schedule, you will need to find some method of recording the many activities, both regular and occasional, that you need to fit in every day. The next chapter introduces you to your many options.

Your Turn

☐ Make up your own takeoff and landing schedule. You may want to download the one from the Get Started page of www.messies.com. If desired, post it where you can refer to it.

☐ What change do you need to make to the way you care for yourself so that you will be able to maintain your energy for your daily schedule?

☐ What could be your inspiration point in your house or office—some spot you keep looking beautiful or some activity that helps you feel successful?

Tips

1. Before you start your day, look at your to-do list.
2. Keep clearly in your mind what you need to do, in what order, and at what time. Schedule the important tasks for a specific time in your daily planner.
3. Create consistent, successful morning and evening routines.
4. Do something nice for yourself every day.
5. Every day take some time out just for you.

Yes or no?

1. Do you keep a central calendar of activities?
2. Are you familiar with the time planners available?
3. Have you been thinking about upgrading the time planning system you use?

If you answer no to questions 1 and 2 and yes to number 3, you are a prime candidate for the information in the next chapter.

---

18 scheduling tools

calendars, pdas, day planners

It's not what you do once in a while; it's what you do day in and day out that makes the difference.

Jenny Craig

As mentioned earlier, our use of time is like having books and a finite amount of shelf space. We can keep all of the books we want as long as we have enough shelves. But there comes a time when we have collected more books than we have shelves to house them. When this happens, we start making decisions about what to keep and what must go.

> **Time Management Choice #8**
> Use the right tools.

When you see that you have filled your time with more than you can do, you need to start the same process of decision making in regards to your time. But we don't use a shelf. We use a (drum roll, please) schedule planner.

An Ivory Weekly Planner

Although today we may use a sophisticated weekly planner, a PDA (personal digital assistant), or a computer-based scheduler, weekly planners are nothing new.

The Wisconsin Historical Museum displays a weekly planner from the 1850s owned by Cassius Fairchild. The pages are made completely of ivory, with the six days of the week (omitting Sunday) labeled at the top. The daily pages are not as thick as the covers that are of a heavier ivory. Only three and a half inches long and one and three-fourths inches wide, the planner fits easily into a shirt pocket. Held together by a pin on the bottom on which the pages swivel out like a fan displaying the labeled pages, each page could be written on with an easily erasable pencil and used week after week. Some markings are still faintly visible.

During the War between the States, Fairchild served with the Wisconsin Voluntary Infantry and was seriously wounded at the battle of Shiloh. We wish we could tell you that a bullet hit him in the chest right on his ivory weekly planner and saved his life, the bullet remaining imbedded in the planner. Good story but not true.

However, this is true. In his civilian life, among other activities, he served as state assemblyman, managed the family businesses, and became chairman of the Democratic party in Wisconsin. His little, heavily used weekly planner probably did save his life repeatedly in more ways than one in his busy life.

Hidden Power of the Planner

Planners have come into their own in today's time crowded world. Ivory has gone out of style. In its place has flowed a myriad of manual paper planners and electronic planners like PDAs and computers. The time planner, whether it is manual or electronic, daily, weekly, or monthly, is valuable for many uses.

Basically planners are used to keep track of things that might otherwise be forgotten or drift away for some other reason. A basic use is for scheduling appointments in an easy-to-access form. You write the name of the person involved, the time, and in some cases the phone contact and address. When you look at that day, the appointment and all of the other scheduled activities for the day stand up in a row without bumping into each other.

But the planner has hidden powers. It is a procrastination breaker. Let's say you have an activity that has no time relevance on your to-do list. Perhaps you need to make a phone call or write a report, something that you don't want to do or that you feel will be unpleasant or difficult. The phone call or the report writing sits on your to-do list undone. The time it needs to be done creeps up on you until you realize you must do the dreaded deed but still you procrastinate.

You can break the cycle of procrastination by moving the job from the to-do list and giving it a specific time on your planner. Somehow having your job next to a definite hour of the day spurs resolve. You will be surprised how scheduling items that are not time specific by their nature on your planner strengthens your determination.

Writing an activity on your planner gives resolve to other items as well, such as break time, family time, lunch, and many other activities that might otherwise become overrun by the tyranny of the immediate.

Low-Tech Planners

Manual (paper) planners come in different formats.

- *One page per day*. This format is good for people who have a lot of notes to go along with their daily schedule.

Some planners even provide two pages for each day to give room for note taking.

- *Two pages per week (week-at-a-glance format).* People who want to keep the activities of the whole week in view prefer this format. It allows them to plan better.
- *Month at a glance (two pages for month).* This format is for people who need to do longer-range planning or need to see farther in advance to make projections.

All of these manual planners come in different sizes.

- *Wallet size.* This planner can be carried in the pocket or purse.
- *Medium size.* About 5 by 8 inches, this planner is for people who want to carry it with them and have space in it for all they need to record.
- *Notebook size.* In this format the pages are designed to carry an 8½- by 11-inch page. Many executives like this size.

The aesthetics of planners vary greatly, from ordinary to beautiful. Carrying cases or holders differ markedly as well. Some use plain paper and some fancy. In short, you can find just about any combination that suits your fancy and need.

Make a trip to the office supply store to find the one that seems best to you. You may have to try several over a period of time before you decide which one you like best. Some people find they need to change planners from time to time to keep from becoming bored or complacent about using one. If you find that you begin to start trying to use your memory to schedule yourself rather than looking in your planner, this is a clue that it is time to make a change to another variety or style of planner. Sometimes the switch needs to take place in the middle of the year.

Manual planner companies offer many add-ons like address books, note pads, goal setters, and other special-needs-based additions.

PDAs

Fast, convenient, compact, and complete, a PDA is one gadget that can do almost anything you could ever want to do, including calculate, take pictures (and send them), keep time and send out alarms, connect you to the Internet, and make phone calls. In the future they will do even more. That is the upside.

The downside is that as a planner, they are more difficult to use because of their small size. Although a PDA keeps individual appointments well, it is hard to read a full day, week, or monthly schedule at a glance.

Also PDAs are easy to lose or damage (25 percent of PDA owners report losing them. The place they are most often lost is in a cab; second is in bars). They can also be stolen and if they are not password protected, sensitive material can be compromised.

People who are not comfortable with technology may feel the learning curve is not worth the effort. Opinions vary wildly about their usefulness. Some people drop the use of a PDA and return to the manual planner, and others shudder at the thought of being without their powerful PDA.

Computers

Computers are popular schedule minders, especially for office workers who are at their computers on a regular basis. Software of various kinds can hold the schedule and alert you with a sound or voice prompt about your appointments or even your entire schedule.

One advantage of using a computer is that it can synchronize with a PDA and with other computers. An additional advantage is that a computer offers maximum flexibility when it comes to your planner. It is easy to change format by simply clicking a button to see your schedule for the day, week, month, or year. You can select and isolate whatever information you want to display. A downside of desktop computers is that they are not portable. And if your computer crashes, you may lose what you have stored.

One Electronic Calendar Example

In addition to some popular calendars like Outlook and iCal (for Macintosh), Google has one of the many calendars available. Google gives clear and accessible support for their calendar on their help page.

You can create many calendars that you use for various purposes that you can overlap when you need an overview of your scheduling. Some of these you can make public when you need to share your schedule with others who can, if you wish, change and add events. You can keep other calendars private, and in some cases you can access other people's or institution's calendars. If your spouse or boss has a Google calendar, you can download their schedule so you can plan your own better. If the place you work, for instance a learning institution, posts its calendar of events on Google, you can download the yearly schedule to help you keep track of holidays, faculty workdays, and other events. A final advantage is that you can access the calendar any place you can access the Internet.

Like many programs, this calendar will send you reminder alerts at specified intervals (an hour, day, or week before an event) by email, SMS text messages, or desktop pop-ups. In addition, it has a great mobile interface if you use the Web on your phone.

True Stories

When you schedule your time, be careful to include your personal interests. Harold Taylor, Canada's top time management expert, tells about an eye-opening event in his time management odyssey. He and his wife loved plays but never seemed to have time to attend. One year when they received their season program agenda, they both got out their planners and scheduled in the ones they wanted to attend. That year, they went. All because they used their planners to make it happen.

One Man's Planner Search

Carlton was excited when he got his company PDA. For days he lived with the manual in his hand at home and at work, everywhere but in the shower. After he learned how to use it, he painstakingly worked at entering all of the phone numbers from his cell phone and all of his appointments in their proper spots.

In his office the next day, he synchronized his PDA with his secretary's computer so nothing would get lost. His alarm alerted him to leave for his first appointment and he arrived in plenty of time. He was loving this new technology.

Unfortunately, he was never able to take notes easily or to enter phone numbers quickly. Appointments with their directions and notes took too long to enter. He started taking manual notes and gathering business cards to enter the information later. Once they were in, they worked great but getting them in was definitely cumbersome.

His secretary was too busy to do the work for him and besides, he had easily done it the old way. So in the end, Carlton returned to using the manual planner because it was easier for him to enter information. He joined many who have found that using the PDA slowed down their productivity. His PDA became a powerful phone book and birthday reminder.

She Never Met a Gadget She Didn't Like

Reba loved her PDA from day one. Learning the graffiti shorthand has been no problem to her and she can enter long texts quickly. Maybe it is because she is twenty-four years old and grew up with technology or maybe it is because she has a natural interest in it.

For her, the PDA is easy. She loves the way it performs when she is away from the office and syncs with her computer when she returns. She is looking for more technology to meet her many needs. She wants a more advanced PDA than the one she now has. She wants to be able to look up things on the Internet, hear directions read to her, sync notes from her computer to the gadget, so that she has at her fingertips notes and information she can share with clients.

Personal Choice

Carlton and Reba are good examples of how people deal with electronic gadgets. For some they are a boon to organizing their life and their productivity. For others they are more trouble than they are worth. Usually, young people, who have grown up with computers, video games, and other electronic equipment, feel at ease with anything new. They move through the learning curve quickly. And many older adults are like this too. But there are people who refuse to try anything new.

Luddites

Long ago, so the legend goes, in a country far away lived a simple lad named Ned Ludd. It was at the beginning of the nineteenth century, and the country was jolly old England. A clumsy sort, Ned Ludd accidentally broke a couple of automated frames in the stocking factory in which he worked. After a while, when machinery broke, it was attributed to poor Ned Ludd.

This took place in the historical context of the industrial revolution when the livelihood of stocking weavers was being threatened by the introduction of laborsaving textile machinery. Eventually the hand weavers started breaking up the threatening machines themselves and saying they were doing so on the orders of General Ned Ludd. These folks became known as Luddites. And since the early 1860s, anyone who opposes automation or technological change is called a Luddite.

While today we may not have people destroying laborsaving devices (except when driven to that point by extreme frustration), there is a definite difference of opinion, among those who are trying to get organized, about using technology. Most people fall somewhere in the middle, using some electronic aids and ignoring others.

Making a Choice

Everybody makes a choice based on personal preference, which often requires a lot of trial and error. Sometimes day planners that worked well in one situation will not work when the situation changes.

One thing is sure. In today's complex world, if you have much to do, you definitely need to find a system that works for you or you will not be able to manage your time successfully.

The next chapter deals with one big problem of poor time management, chronic lateness.

Your Turn

☐ If you already have technology gadgets that work well for you in scheduling your time, commit to using them consistently.

☐ If you are looking to upgrade, ask friends what works well for them. Visit office supply stores and look at their paper planners. See what electronics stores have that might meet your needs. Peruse the Internet to see what is available. Consider some of the powerful computer software available. In other words, take seriously the search for the correct planning devices for you.

Tips

1. Use the same planner for your home and office life.
2. Purchase an annual wall calendar and put on it important prescheduled activities, such as the school calendar, vacation times, birthdays, and so on. Even if you schedule on a PDA, a wall calendar acts as a backup and communication with others.
3. Color code different types of activities on the calendar.
4. Free your mind by entering all of your commitments in your planner.
5. If you are often away from your base, carry your to-do list in your planner.

True or false?

1. I know my lateness inconveniences others.
2. I try to be on time but somehow I often don't make it.
3. I hate waiting, so I plan to be right on time or a little late.

If you answered true to any these, you need to conquer your chronic lateness problem. Read on to find out how.

---

19 chronic lateness

understanding and curing the problem

> Unfaithfulness in the keeping of an appointment is an act of clear dishonesty. You may as well borrow a person's money as his time.
>
> Horace Mann

It had always been Alan's habit to be late to appointments, work, social engagements, church, and any other commitment that had a starting time. When his wife complained about it, he took the philosophical high road, claiming that he was "living in the now" and could not, should not, plan ahead. He focused completely on whatever he was doing at the time and could not seem to re-focus on his next item of business. Since he did not look ahead, he had no internal pressure to move from what he was doing to his next commitment.

"Nothing starts until I get there," was Alan's favorite quip to excuse his chronic lateness. He failed to consider how his habit affected his wife, friends, and those who had to wait on him for meetings. Usually his wife was embarrassed by their lateness, his friends got annoyed, and his co-workers dreaded having to review what had happened at a meeting before he arrived. He overlooked all of this until one day when his lateness affected him in a way he never forgot.

That was the day he missed the sailing of the cruise ship on which his extended family was celebrating his grandmother's ninetieth birthday. He and his wife stood alone on the dock beside their suitcases watching the ship on the horizon. Literally they had missed the boat.

Causes of Lateness

Like Alan, some people make it a habit never to be punctual. The reasons for this vary. Here are some of them:

- *Poor time estimate.* Some people, probably because of an attention deficit that trips them up, fail to realize how much time things take. If asked to estimate when a minute has passed, their guesses fall far short of reality. So they underestimate how long it will take to get ready in the morning or drive to work or write a report. Because they have not timed their activities and do not realize in any other way how long it takes them to do these activities, they don't learn from their mistakes. Many people who do not have a problem with lateness have an internal clock and can "feel" the passage of time accurately and because of experience can predict how long things will take.
- *Misperception of the passage of time.* Alan might look at the clock and see he has five minutes before he has to leave, so he decides to do one more thing. When he looks up at the clock again, he is surprised to see that fifteen, instead of five, minutes have passed, and he is tardy again.
- *Careless planning.* Free spirits may be late because they failed to write down the address or get directions beforehand. They like to wing it.

- *Spotty memory for details*. Some people are frequently late because of a spotty memory problem. They work diligently at getting ready on time but overlook time-consuming peripheral details. They get dressed but don't figure in enough time for putting on jewelry and makeup, brushing hair and teeth, and so on. When they should be walking out the door, they are still getting ready.

    In the same way, they may fix a wonderful dinner, but it's all ready and cooling off while they rush about setting the table, putting ice in the glasses, pouring drinks, and handling things that should have been done earlier. Again and again, failure to count important peripheral activities as part of the time usage makes people rush to be on time and frequently to fail.

- *Need for pressure*. For some people, the rush of adrenaline is an important part of meeting time deadlines. Because they are easygoing by nature, they use the pressure of a deadline to rally their forces. They use this tactic when completing projects, such as writing reports, or for just getting out the door in the morning. After a while they come to rely on that rush to move them to action. The problem is that they often shave it too close and miss the mark.

    People who need this adrenaline rush may even add to the time pressure by seeing things that need to be done, and they take "just a minute" to do them. They may stop to polish the mirror, put away some clutter, clear the kitchen counter, or sort socks before they go out the door. Doing these quickie jobs seems so right to the person empowered by adrenaline but it cuts into his or her progress and frequently makes the person late.

- *Ignore the need for cushion time*. Somewhat akin to the person who fails to take peripherals into account is the person who does not leave appropriate cushion time when planning activities. When they need to meet the shuttle to the airport at the hotel, they may fail to include in their plans the time it takes to reach the waiting shuttle from the room. Instead, they leave the room at the time the shuttle is to leave. It is typical for these people to underestimate commute time or to be overly optimistic about the traffic and thus arrive late.

- *Hindered by messiness.* Messiness is a common reason for lateness. It may be that pieces of clothing or personal care items are lost and the person must take time looking for them, or the things the person needs to take along on a trip or to the office are so scattered that it takes time to assemble them.

- *Dislike of waiting.* Some people who hate "dead" time push things to the last minute to avoid being idle. They consider that waiting for an appointment is a huge waste of time, so they arrive late. They consider themselves capable time managers and wonder why others are willing to squander time by getting places on time or early.

- *Self-absorption.* Some people are chronically late because they want to make a splashy entrance once the festivities or meeting has begun. They are the center of attention as they offer apologies or are brought up to date on what they missed. Those who are inconvenienced, because they have had to wait, feel disrespected and unimportant.

Changing the Lateness Habit

When they realized they had missed the cruise, Alan was heartbroken and his wife was in tears. Alan could not justify his lateness habit any longer and he vowed to change.

The first thing he did was to write a letter of apology to his family and his grandmother. Then he took steps to change his ways of doing things. He decided he would be more careful about the commitments he made. Previously he had said yes to most everything. If at the time of the event, he didn't really want to go, he would drag his feet and end up being late.

Alan began to rely heavily on his calendar. If there was an event to which he really wanted to go, he first checked his calendar to see whether realistically he had the time to put it on his schedule.

He began another habit. Each time he wrote down the time of an event, he also noted in his planner the time he needed to leave the office or his home to arrive on time. That way, the first notation that got his attention was the leaving time, not the time the event was to begin.

To help keep himself on track with his decisions, he made a commitment to his wife and told her what he planned to do. He asked her to hold him accountable.

For the next thirty days he tried to put his plan into practice. He started saying no tactfully to some invitations. He did not accept a leadership position in an organization to which he belonged. He stopped going places he didn't really want to go. In other words, he became more discriminating about some of the routine obligations that he did not like doing. Additionally he became a stickler about estimating commute time.

Instead of dreading being early to things, he took a book or project with him in case he had to wait. Slowly he became a model of punctuality.

Alan grew to like this new way of life. His family had forgiven him (though he may not have fully forgiven himself). His wife was happier and so were his kids. And he got more done with less stress than ever before.

When Alan changed his behavior, he changed his habit of being late. The eighth time management choice concerns powerful, life-changing habits, which will be dealt with in the next chapter.

Your Turn

☐ Check any of the reasons given that might be responsible for times when you are late.

☐ poor time estimate

Suggestion: Time your habitual activities so you can predict better in the future. Write them down.

☐ misperception of time passing

Suggestion: Avoid the "I'll do one more thing" habit.

☐ careless planning

Suggestion: Make the effort to keep track of important details.

☐ spotty memory for detail

Suggestion: Make a list ahead of time and check it off as you go.

☐ need for pressure

Suggestion: Set a false earlier deadline and work toward it.

☐ ignoring the need for cushion time

Suggestion: Make it a habit to allow "cushion time" in your life.

☐ hindered by messiness

Suggestion: Attack the clutter in your life.

☐ dislike of waiting

Suggestion: Take work with you to fill in waiting time.

☐ self-absorption

Suggestion: Realize that you are inconveniencing others and damaging your own reputation.

☐ Name the steps you'll take to be on time more consistently.

Tips

1. In your planner, circle the time to leave for your appointment as well as the time the appointment starts.
2. Designate a specific place to leave small, important items, such as your keys, wallet, purse, glasses, and the like. Always leave these items in their appointed place.
3. Fill your gas tank before it is nearly empty so you won't be forced to stop for gas on the way to an appointment.
4. Plan for the morning the night before.
5. Make a new commitment to be on time.
6. Leave very early to arrive early. Use your time cushion to catch up on reading.

True or false?

1. I like the freedom of doing things spontaneously.
2. I struggle to keep on top of things.
3. If I improved my time management habits, my life would run more smoothly.

If you answered true to any of the above, pay close attention to the next important chapter.

---

20 creating powerful habits

surefire methods that work

There is no more miserable human being than one in whom nothing is habitual.

William James

First we form habits, then they form us. Conquer your bad habits or they will conquer you.

Rob Gilbert

To get organized and stay organized, you need three things: the correct systems, the correct tools, and the correct habits. One without the others will not work. For example, you can have the best filing system in the world and the best filing cabinet money can buy, but if you don't have the habit of filing on a regular basis, your papers will still be a mess.

Developing good habits is a powerful way to enhance your life. Those who have developed good habits usually follow them so automatically they fail to tell others about how important they are. Many others don't develop good habits because they don't realize the benefits they will enjoy and because new habits are hard to establish.

Organized people work dispassionately. That frees them from a lot of stress. Disorganized people wear themselves out by investing emotion in the things they have to do. They work while saying, "I hate making the bed every day" or "Unloading the dishwasher is such a drag." The way to take the emotion out of doing what you need to do regularly is to make the activity into a habit.

How to Develop Good Habits

There are two motivators for taking the time and trouble to create a new habit. One is the desire for gain. You want to improve your life, maybe get a promotion, be seen in a more positive light, be able to accomplish more, and feel better about what you get done.

The other reason is far more powerful; it is the desire to avoid pain. When you spend precious time looking for something, when you consistently turn reports in late, or when you lose a job because you are late for an interview, you may realize the need to develop habits to help you stay organized.

The way to develop a habit is to commit yourself, by an act of your will, to doing the desired habit for twenty-one days. Twenty-one days is considered the time needed for developing a habit, though of course it varies from person to person and habit to habit. At first, the new activity may be unpleasant and you may have to force yourself to follow through with your vow. As you do it day after day, your dislike and dread

Habit is habit, and not to be flung out of the window by any man, but coaxed downstairs one step at a time.
—Mark Twain
The Tragedy of Pudd'nhead Wilson

will diminish. Soon you will just be annoyed by having to do it. One day you will do it without emotion. Eventually you will do it so automatically you may not even notice you have done it.

What Habits to Develop

All habits are by their nature short activities that are done over and over again in a consistent way. Here are some good habits to develop to help you stay organized.

At the Office

- Check your planner at the end of every workday to see what is on the schedule for tomorrow.
- Give your office the once-over as you leave for the day. Make it like you want it to be when you return.
- Write phone messages in the designated place each time (no more scraps of paper).
- Write your appointments in your planner as soon as you make them.
- Consult your planner before making a commitment.
- Confirm appointments in advance.
- Return material to the file immediately after using it.
- Stash important emails in the pertinent folder as soon as you read them.

In the Home

- Hang up your clothes or put them in a hamper as you undress.
- Write appointments on your calendar or planner.
- Keep street directions in a certain spot so they are easily found.

- Put things by the front door that you will need to take with you in the morning.
- Read your mail daily with a trash can and shredder nearby.
- Write down phone messages for other family members, rather than trying to remember to tell them.
- Leave your house or a room the way you want it to look when you return.
- Leave the house fifteen minutes earlier than you think you need to when you go to an appointment.

Ruth's Experience

Traffic was bumper-to-bumper as Ruth hurried to work. She had hit the snooze button one too many times, showered quickly, grabbed a bite, looked for her purse and keys, scooped up her papers, and scooted out. She breathed a sigh of relief as she stepped into the office just as the clock showed eight. Putting her things on the chair, she listened to her messages and wrote the information on sticky notes she found on her desk. At 10:15 she remembered to look at her calendar. It was a good thing she did because she had a meeting with her boss scheduled for 10:30 to present a report she had written. The report had been completed and was with her other papers on the chair. She had intended to make a few additions but it was too late now so she dug it out, looked it over, and scrambled down the hall. Whew!

> Motivation is what gets you started. Habit is what keeps you going.
> —Jim Rylan

All day long she was slightly behind the eight ball. Fortunately everything worked out okay but it had taken a toll on her emotionally. Ruth decided to make some serious changes in how she lived. First, she set the alarm clock for fifteen minutes earlier and put it across the room so she wouldn't be tempted to press the snooze button. Next she got a telephone log for her phone records. Finally, she decided to check her planner the first thing every morning.

> A nail is driven out by another nail. Habit is overcome by habit.
> —Desiderius Erasmus

Once she moved the clock and reset the alarm, she felt good about what she had done so far. At work, with her phone message log beside her answering machine, she had no trouble using it regularly. Two behavioral habits she wanted to create were to put her purse and keys by the front door at night and to remember to check her planner as soon as she entered her office. While she was developing these budding habits, she used prompts. On the table by the door she put a card that said, "Put purse here." When she left work in the afternoon, she left her planner open to the next day's page on her desk chair so she had to pick it up before she could sit down each morning.

The four changes Ruth made, two that were behavioral in nature (actions she needed to alter) and two that were mechanical (nonpersonal), changed significantly her performance and her self-esteem. She learned the power that a few simple habit changes could have on her life.

Don't be misled by the simplicity of the new habits. These straightforward alterations will save large amounts of time because they will solve problems before they develop.

The Big Three

Many small habits, such as those Ruth made specifically tailored to her situation, are important and can significantly impact lives for the better. However, there are three powerful general habits that, if applied, would take care of the majority of time management issues.

- *The thirty-second rule*. If a job takes thirty seconds or less, do it immediately. This applies to such tasks as hanging up your coat, putting away the book bag, taking the garbage can back to its place, rinsing out the sink after dinner, wiping up a spill, and discarding junk mail.

- *If you get it out, put it back—quickly*. Everybody plans to put it back *eventually*. In that delay is the flaw. While it sits out, it becomes clutter and will take time away from you in the future.

  Also, put it back *exactly* where it belongs. The book belongs back on the shelf not on the top of the bookcase. The clothes belong in the closet not flung over the door. The folder should be returned to the file not put on the desk. Close is not good enough. In chapter 3 we introduced this saying: Stow as you go! This is a habit everyone who wants to succeed at time management must practice.

- *Keep surfaces clear*. This is the big blockbuster habit of time management. At home and in the office, on the floor, desk, table, chair, everywhere—commit to maintaining appropriately bare surfaces. Homes and offices need space to breathe and a cluttered surface stifles that freedom. When you clear areas so they contain only what should be there, it energizes you to action and keeps "stuff" from hindering what you want to do.

The next chapter deals with how to organize your space at home and keep surfaces clear, and chapter 22 deals with organizing your business or home office.

Habits for the Home

A good life is made by good habits. The following are good habits that when repeated will become a way of life for you and those with whom you share your home.

You and your family could make a kind of game out of reading and committing to the list of new habits you want to develop. Make a copy of the list below, cut it apart so that each habit is on a separate strip of paper, and put the strips in a jar. At the dinner table take turns pulling a strip out of the jar, reading it, and discussing whether the family has this habit already. If it's a habit your family wants to work on, you may want to make a poster out of the statement and hang it in an appropriate place in the house. Or you may just want to repeat the appropriate ones as reminders. If you live alone, adapt the list to your situation.

In our house we hang up the towels neatly after bathing.

In our house we put what we need to take with us the next day by the front door the night before.

In our house we don't drop our things when we come in the door. We put them where they belong.

In our house we put dirty clothes into the hamper as soon as we take them off.

In our house we make our beds before we leave our room in the morning.

In our house we put dishes into the dishwasher, not in the sink.

In our house we take responsibility for completing the chores assigned to us.

In our house we don't complain about our responsibilities.

In our house we always flush the toilet immediately after use.

In our house we put away toys, games, tools, and stuff as soon as we finish with them.

In our house we don't leave things out just because we plan to get back to the project later.

In our house we wash, dry, fold, and put away our clothes as one continuous job.

In our house we make sure all trash goes into the trash basket.

In our house we value each other and the contribution each makes.

In our house we keep our closets and drawers neat.

In our house we use the team concept. Each person does his or her part to support the others.

In our house we are willing to help others when necessary because we are a team.

In our house we don't leave messes or create work for others.

In our house we don't boss others. We focus on our own responsibilities.

In our house we talk kindly to each other.

In our house we try to think ahead to solve problems before they happen.

In our house we pay attention to maintaining beauty.

In our house we push our chairs up to the table when we are finished with our meal.

In our house we use one bath towel for a week.

In our house we change our bed sheets every two weeks.

In our house we strive to complete projects and clean up expeditiously.

In our house the person who uses the last sheet of toilet paper puts a new roll on the dispenser.

In our house we discard (give to charity or—gasp!—throw out) an old one when we bring in a new tool, book, toy, or other item.

In our house we leave the bathroom vanity clear of makeup and shaving gear.

In our house we write what we need at the store on the whiteboard.

In our house we move the garbage cans out of sight after they have been emptied at the curb.

Your Turn

☐ What *mechanical* changes (like putting a clock in each room) can you make *at home* that will improve how you use your time?

☐ What *mechanical* changes (such as turning your chair away from the door) can you make *at work* that will improve how you use your time?

☐ What *personal* changes (like adhering to the thirty-second rule) can you make *at home* that will improve the way you use your time?

☐ What *personal* changes (like replacing items as soon as they are used) can you make *at work* that will improve the way you use your time?

Habits for the Solo Worker

Whether you are an entrepreneur or work for a company at home, these habits will be the backbone for your success.

At my work I check my calendar before I start my day.
At my work I put things back where they belong after use.
At my work I put files back immediately when possible.
At my work I keep a running tally of needed office supplies.
At my work I create a regular time to do banking.

Habits for Office Workers

Your habits may include those for the solo worker and a few more that apply to working with others.

At my work we respect each other's time.
At my work we try to help each other when we can.
At my work we ask before we move somebody else's papers.
At my work we ask before we schedule appointments for other people.
At my work we respect co-workers' break times.
At my work we make sure we notify purchasing when we need supplies.
At my work we don't take commonly used items from their place without asking.
At my work we respect the time, space, and belongings of others.

Tips

1. Create a routine you want to do every day at the same time. Don't vary it and it will become a habit.
2. Set aside a specific time during the day to make decisions about incoming mail (both paper and email) and make a habit of using this time for this purpose.
3. If you habitually do the same thing, you will keep getting the same results. If you want change, you must change something.
4. Wake up earlier to get a jump start on your day.

21 organize your space at home

de-stress your life and free yourself

We shape our dwellings, and afterwards our dwellings shape us.

Winston Churchill

Do not keep anything in your home that you do not know to be useful or believe to be beautiful.

William Morris

Clutter is not a friend of efficient time use. You waste time when you have to look for things, when things are inconveniently stored, or when you have to take extra steps because things have not been put back in the proper place. Clutter slows us down, confuses us, and discourages us from trying to accomplish things.

Simplify

Dejunking is one of the surest ways of empowering your use of time. Step out of mindless collecting into simplicity.

Over the years, poets and philosophers have warned us against having too much stuff. Walt Whitman speaks of "the mania of owning things" and George Santayana says it this way: "Private wealth I should decline, or any sort of personal possessions, because they would take away my liberty."

Time Management Choice #10

Organize your space.

Don Aslett lays it on the line with this straightforward admonition: "The number one, the very first step to becoming a 'more doer,' a high producer, is to stop accumulating and start eliminating. In other words, dejunk!"

You don't have to think about it very long before you realize that we spend large amounts of time buying, storing, moving, cleaning, putting away, and trying to organize our stuff. It is overwhelming because we just have w-a-a-a-y too much. Some of it is pretty useless. Some of it may be "good" but it is not good for us at this time. Besides, we don't have room in our lives for all the "good" things that come our way. So decisions of what to do with the excess have to be faced fearlessly.

Dealing with Clutter

Of course there are reasons we have so much—good reasons at that.

We acquired something because:

"It was a bargain."

"It was free!"

"I inherited it from a loved one."

"I love this kind of thing."

"I love to shop."

"I moved it from a large house to this smaller place."

We keep the items that are adding to the clutter in our homes because:

"I've had it since I was a child."

"It reminds me of my dear Aunt Sally."

"I wouldn't be able to replace it."

"It is unique."

"I don't want to offend the giver."

"I paid good money for it."

"I may find a use for it someday."

"I'm not ready right now."

"It's still good."

"It brings back memories."

These excuses are not reason enough to hinder the wonderful opportunities in your life. If you streamline your belongings, you will de-stress your life and free yourself to have more time for doing more of what you really want to do. Though it is difficult, you can do it. There are several ways to declutter your surroundings.

Store It Elsewhere

Storing the clutter elsewhere is a quick and effective method that is a variation of the Mount Vesuvius method described on the Messies Anonymous website, www.messies.com. Use it to clear surfaces (include the floor and all furniture as surfaces) and store your things quickly in an organized way.

> Keeping house is like threading beads on a string with no knot at the end.

Buy cardboard storage boxes (15-by-12-by-10 inches) at your office supply store. It's most economical to buy packages of ten. Since they aren't expensive, buy as many as you need to accomplish the decluttering of your house. They are white boxes that can be collapsed flat for storage when you empty them later. Or put them in the recycle bin when you are finished using them.

On a piece of white paper, write the name of a category of items you want to remove from your living areas but keep in your possession. Tape the label to the front of the box and begin filling it with excess items. Your categories may include sports equipment, knickknacks, snapshots and albums, books, kids' school papers, and the like.

Now store the filled boxes out of the way in some appropriate place. As you stack them one on top of the other against a wall, they won't take up much floor space and because they are white and uniform they will not be an eyesore. You may (or may not) want to minimize the writing on the front to a small card, number them, and make a list of what is in each box. If you store the boxes in several places, such as the garage, attic, and basement, keep a list of where each box is located. Write their location on your master list and store it in your file cabinet.

Give It Away

As you go about your decluttering, you will find things that you are willing to part with. My suggestion is to take them to the nearest charity or, better yet, call one to come to the house and pick up your donations. (If you know they are coming, you will follow through more readily.) If you decide to offer things to friends, set a deadline for their acceptance. After a certain date (written on the box), if your friend has not picked it up, give it to a charity. Write the timetable for giving things away on your to-do master list and store the list in (or on the front of) your file cabinet.

Sell It

For items you would like to sell, put ads in the newspaper or on the Internet. Or plan a yard sale. Sometimes you can let a possession go more easily to individuals who pay money for it, because you can see they value it enough to buy it. Again, set a date. If you don't follow through on your plan to have a sale, you may use this "good idea" as an excuse to keep the stuff. A good Internet site to list your for-sale items at no charge is www.craigslist.com.

Toss It

Undoubtedly you will come across things that are not good enough to keep, sell, or even give away. Throw them out and take the bag or box out to the trash immediately. Remember, your goal is to dejunk the house so you don't want to keep bags of trash in the house even for a short time. If you find it painful to throw things out even if they are junk, put the things in a box or bag and ask an ally to do the final coup de grâce by removing it from the house.

Talk Seriously to Yourself

As you try to decide the course to take in your effort to de-clutter, ask yourself the following questions.

- *Is it valuable enough to keep*? There are a few things that are an important part of our past, that are valuable from a sentimental standpoint. They should be kept but perhaps in a storage area. Other things that are monetarily valuable but are not personally important should be stored away or sold.
- *Is it useful at this time*? Get rid of all broken and outdated items. It's highly unlikely that your dreams of resur-

recting them will come true. Face the music and move them on quickly. If you must keep them, corral them into one of those cardboard storage boxes and label it "broken things."

If you are a very imaginative and creative person, you will undoubtedly think of a way to use almost anything like stockings with runs, plastic butter dishes, and empty picture frames. Don't put that pressure on yourself. Face the fact that you have more ideas than you can, or should, put into practice. If you discard an item, you release your responsibility to find some use for it.

If you are a craft person, you need to restrict your supplies, or they will turn your house into a storeroom. Boundaries and restraint are necessary when it comes to keeping items that may be useful later.

- *Is the recycling concept a problem?* Even if you are a strong environmentalist, don't save clutter in your house until you find the perfect home for it. Eventually it will have to be removed from your house anyway. In the meantime, don't turn your house into a landfill.

When you hold on to things, you are keeping them from being made into other items. Recycling will save on energy that would be used to produce items from virgin materials. So use whatever recycling system is available in your area. Set up an easy-to-use method of collecting in your house. Don't wear yourself out by overdoing every detail, such as researching to find the right charity. Your throwaways will begin to pile up waiting for collection if you don't have a well-oiled plan for moving them out, such as bins in the garage to collect bottles, cans, newspapers, etc. When the bins are full, it's time to go to the recycling center. Done is better than perfect.

- *Is this item a burden for me?* Half-finished projects fit into this category. These are often crafts, like a painting you never finished or an afghan stopped because you needed more yarn and couldn't find more of the same color. Your craft clutter may be materials you collected long ago when you used to sew or quilt, or supplies that are left over from remodeling jobs that you wanted to use but never got back to. When you allow items to sit around that remind you of tasks you intended to do, they become a burden, destroying your peace. It's best to get rid of them.

Think hard about keeping things that depress you when you see them. Because they accuse you of procrastination each time you see them, they drag down your spirit. Clear them from your living area, using one of the methods mentioned above.

Moving On

What a relief! All of the clutter (or at least most of it) has been removed from the house. It's looking good! Maybe this is one of those times to say whoopee! and plan to give yourself a celebratory reward.

Gather Like Things

Already your time, your mind, and your emotions have been freed up, but still something may not be quite right yet. Your time management is hindered by the fact that what you are keeping is still not well organized.

Items you use are scattered about the house. When you want to fix or build something, you go for the hammer in the garage, the screwdriver in the utility room, nails in the basement, and so on. Something as simple as cleaning the house requires you to get cleaner from under the sink, dust cloths from the hall closet, mop and bucket from the laundry room, and on and on it goes.

One cardinal rule of organizing has been broken—nay, shattered—and you need to fix it. Things that are alike or perform the same function must be collected and stored side by side. In other words, they must be huddled together physically. When they are, you save a lot of time in two ways: you don't have to look for where each item might be stored and you don't have to take as many steps to get it. If you group like things together, making them readily accessible, your use of time will zoom forward on the graph of efficiency.

I cleaned my house yesterday. Sure wish you could have seen it.

One big advantage of grouping things together is that you will see how many duplicates you have. A few things like scissors and cellophane tape should be kept in rooms all around the house. Except in those cases, you need to discard excess staplers, glue guns, pens, unwanted shoes, duplicate books, and other surplus items.

Storage

As you function in your now decluttered house with things that are alike grouped together, you notice that one final issue needs to be addressed. Where are you going to store these different groupings? The issue of storage is an important one. The answer has several parts but is pretty simple. Follow these guidelines as much as possible in the space you have for storage.

- *Locate the items close to where they are going to be used.* Obviously, pots and pans reside near the stove; dishes are stored near the dishwasher. Towels are stored in or close to the bathroom, as are toiletries. Building tools go in the garage or basement and garden tools are stored in the shed outside. Though this concept is simple, sometimes we have to be creative to fit everything into the spaces we have for storage.

- *Place the items at the proper level.* If they are used often, make them easily accessible, often at arm's length at a height between the hips and the head. The less often they are used, the more inaccessible they can become, stored up high or down low on shelves in the house or, in some cases, archived into the attic or basement.
- *Place items in baskets, boxes, or other appropriate containers.* Label the container clearly on the side that faces out. That way you and those who share the house with you can easily see where to find what is needed and, just as important, where to return it.

Once your house is in order like this, you will be organized and efficient, and your frustration will decline.

Keeping It Up

Anybody who has at one time gotten organized knows that the really serious challenge comes in maintaining the organization you have created. The first big kahuna of maintenance is habit, especially the habit that can't be mentioned too often: you already know that when you get it out, you must put it back—immediately or absolutely as soon as possible.

Second, you need a few simple schedules. For cleaning and laundry, write your schedule on a calendar, paper or computer-based planner, or use the Messies Anonymous Flipper System (go to www.messies.com for info) or any other system that works for you.

The chief problem with laundry is that it is not done often enough. The laundry schedule can be as simple as planning to do a load a day that you vow to do from beginning to end in that one calendar day. In this plan, the dirty clothes start out in the hamper at the beginning of the day and end up put away in closet, drawer, or shelf the same day. Nothing is left in baskets, washer, or dryer overnight. It's a good idea to train the members of your family to do their own laundry and give each a day in which the washing machine is theirs. Of course, when they do their own wash, it means they also dry it and put everything away in one day.

Finally, make it a ritual to spend fifteen minutes a day decluttering anything that may have crept out into your well-managed living space. Make it a family affair and even a game. You will be surprised at how much can be done in that short designated time.

Kim's Solution

Kim and Randolf had been seeing each other for about two weeks. She felt she should invite him over or at least have him pick her up at her house, but it was just too junky.

Kim spent much of her time fighting the clutter battle and losing. She came home from eight hours of work with little energy to clean her place and pick up the clutter. How would she have time to get it ready for Randolf's visit? It seemed impossible.

Spurred by the excitement of her new relationship, she was determined to get a grip on the solution once and for all. She bought a supply of boxes and a broad-tipped black marker. She set up the boxes, labeled them and, reaching toward them like an octopus, dropped the various items into their respective boxes. She started out with boxes labeled "sweaters," "shoes," "books," "electrical stuff," "magazines," "office supplies," "unopened mail," and "CDs." Before long other groupings formed and boxes were needed for them. As each box became full, she put the top on it, keeping track of the number of boxes she was collecting.

A whole lot of things went into a large black leaf bag she had brought in to take the trash and broken things she knew would be there. In another large bag, she put items she did not like or had outgrown, or they were duplicates, and planned to donate them to a local charity. It took five hours to clear the living room, longer than she thought it would because, as she worked, she found she agonized over the decisions she was making. Then she carried the boxes into the rooms in which the items inside belonged and would later be stored.

Wow! This looks almost presentable, she thought. And then she did what she had not been able to do in years; she gave herself the gift of hiring a housecleaner to clean "just the living room, bathroom, kitchen, and dining room," she explained, keeping the back rooms closed off.

When she looked around that evening, she saw her house in a different light. Remembering beautiful pictures in the home decor magazines she had always loved, she set about to beautify her surroundings by rearranging furniture, discarding what had outlived its day, and buying decorative pieces that pulled together her color scheme. Following the magazine example, she added flowers. When she was satisfied, she invited Randolf over for coffee and later for dinner.

Week after week she continued to work the same system for the other rooms in the house until all of the rooms were organized and the items she kept were stored.

Months later Kim was able to say a happy yes! when Randolf asked her to marry him, without having to worry about his moving into the house.

Because she followed basic maintenance procedures, Kim could spend time enjoying her newfound love and planning for the wedding instead of grappling daily with clutter.

> Order is the shape upon which beauty depends.
> —Pearl S. Buck

Kim had started her organizing project to relieve the pain of living with clutter but she continued it because she loved the beauty and the freedom it gave her to live a fulfilling life.

In many ways our offices face the same issues as our homes. This is the subject of the next chapter.

Your Turn

☐ Kim had a special reason for fixing up her house. What is your reason? Would organizing the house help to relieve your time crunch?

☐ If you keep too much, what are your chief reasons for doing so?

Tips

1. Get a bigger trash can.
2. Keep surfaces clear.
3. When you take something out from where it belongs, put it back ASAP.
4. Don't overbuy. Discard one item each time you buy another.
5. Take the last five minutes of your day to straighten up your home.

True or false?

1. Things I need are often within easy reach in my office.
2. I have only the things I need for business in my office.
3. My office is well-equipped for my work.

If you answered true to all of these statements, you will enjoy chapter 22 knowing you are on top of things. If you answered false to any of them, you will benefit from the information.

---

22 organize your business or home office

ensure maximum productivity

There is a difference between being neat and being organized. You can have an organized office that looks messy because you are working on a project that requires you to have a lot of pieces out as you work. On the other hand, you can have a neat looking office because all of the surfaces are clear and yet not know where things are.

An organized office is one in which you can quickly and consistently put your hand on what you need. If it looks good as well, that's a plus because it makes visitors think more highly of the owner of the office and you will enjoy it more. Right or wrong, the client of a doctor, lawyer, insurance agent, or any businessperson feels more confident in the professional's ability if he or she has a neat office.

Your level of success in life is directly proportional to your level of planning for it.

As you know, any time plan for organizing your office needs the correct system, tools, and habits.

A Paper-Flow System

Paul had a system but it didn't work well.

One day when a new customer came in to sign up for her gym membership, Paul was on the phone. When he got off the phone and assessed her need, he began preparing a membership packet. He opened the bottom desk drawer and pulled out a paper that needed to go in the membership packet. Then he turned around to retrieve a paper from a folder on the credenza and put it in the packet. Turning around again he stood up to retrieve a paper from the shelf above his head. Back in his seat, he leaned to his right to retrieve a paper on the far corner of his desk. Finally he walked behind the customer to get an envelope in which to put the packet. He attached his business card to the group of papers and handed them to the prospective member. Paul had made six significant movements to assemble the packet.

At that point a lightbulb went on in Paul's brain. Why hadn't it occurred to him before? He could keep all of the papers in separate files in a file drawer beside his desk so that he could easily assemble the specific papers needed for the selected program of each individual.

When you find you have to reach over things, through things, and behind things to accomplish a task, you are wasting time. It may seem it only takes a few seconds, but repeated over and over, it adds up over the day, week, and month. Because we don't notice all of the little pieces of time that we waste inadvertently, we don't realize how much valuable time we are squandering. We think time loss happens in large chunks, but most significant time loss actually happens in small increments.

Pay attention to the number of steps and movements you make to get a job done. Determine if some of these could be eliminated, were you better organized. See what changes you can make that will solve the small time leaks in your office.

A Space Plan

Randy needed a different kind of system. He was losing time because he so often had to look for things. Randy inherited an office from the account manager at the radio station where he was hired. The beauty of it was the bank of cabinets on the wall behind his desk, which held all of his papers, products, and supplies. His office always looked nice because everything was encapsulated behind those cabinet doors. The problem was he had never decided how he was going to organize the shelves, so the cabinets turned out to be something of a black hole. Anything could be anywhere.

One of the most stressful and frustrating things in the world is to know you have something and not be able to find it. The stress gets worse if your boss or staff need it right away, and the rising panic makes you even less efficient in your search.

Randy solved his problem by drawing a schematic of the shelves. He decided books he seldom needed should go high on the top shelves. Urgent paperwork was placed close at hand behind him. Papers and samples for his accounts were to the right and forms to the left on mid-level shelves. Reading materials and memos went to the bottom shelves, along with his personal items, such as his lunch, thermos, and gym clothes.

Do the right thing, not the easy thing.

To remember his organization plan, he wrote the name of the grouping for each section and stuck it in the appropriate location.

The lesson we learn from Randy is to take time to make a plan and to rearrange things to fit that plan. Although it takes more time to set up initially, when you can put your hands on what you need instantly, the organizing time is well worth it.

To be efficient and make the best use of your space, create a space plan and add labels so you don't forget where everything belongs.

Functional Furnishings

A successful business must have the right furniture in the right places, so it is important that your furniture support your daily activity and that it fit the space available.

Think ahead about what kind of furniture will fit your office space and shape. A long, narrow office will do better with lateral files that fit against the wall rather than vertical files that stick out into your floor space. Having files that work well and are placed properly is often the key to good use of time in the office.

Choose your desk carefully. If you don't have much room, you may want to use a piece of wide shelving that can rest on a couple of two-drawer filing cabinets. When placing your desk, locate it so there is no glare on your computer screen.

And while we're talking about desks, here are some pointers for your desktop: plan to clear off your desk at the end of the day, and try to avoid having the stapler, hole punch, candy dish, cups for pencils and pens, family picture, and other clutter on the desk surface if possible.

Be sure your chair is comfortable. Think about what kind of chair works for you. Do you need a low-back chair with no arms, so you can type, or a high-backed executive-type chair? Do you want something ergonomically correct or just soft and comfortable? Deciding on the proper chair is one of your most important decisions.

If possible, place a bookshelf in your office to hold reading material, binders, and books that would otherwise have no storage spot. If you have extra room on the bookshelf, use it to locate stacking trays, office supplies, and pictures or knickknacks.

Credenzas are optional. If you have the room and the need, a credenza is another shelf and storage area. If space is short and you have to choose between a credenza and a bookshelf, go for the bookshelf. You get more use out of the floor space it occupies.

In a productive office, lighting must be adequate. Dim lighting will slow down your work and may drive you out of the office to another room where the lighting is better. On the other hand, when lighting is too bright, it will wear you out and make you want to leave the office, perhaps without realizing what the problem is.

Some people do well with bulletin boards. A list of needed phone numbers, up-to-date announcements, awards, thank-you cards, and decorative material artistically displayed can make bulletin boards an enhancement to an office. Some people mistakenly use bulletin boards as a replacement for a pile, sticking all kinds of jumbled material on them. Before long these papers become out of date and useless. When used like that, bulletin boards become an eyesore. If that happens to you, get rid of the bulletin board.

Productive Equipment for Home Offices

It may seem obvious, but for a home office you need to have basic equipment, which for most people is a computer, printer/scanner/copier (and/or fax). You need a telephone with accessories that meet your requirements. Make sure your connection to the Internet is as fast and easy as you need. Depending on the type of work your company does, other equipment may be necessary.

Be aware that for your office equipment, you will need appropriate surfaces—desks or tables—located near proper outlets. Some pieces of equipment can be placed on shelves, a credenza, or file cabinet top. Try to leave your desktop as free as possible.

Well-Chosen Furniture

Jack was excited. His last kid had moved out and he had finally gotten around to moving his law practice fully into his home office. He had the room painted beautifully and hung his plaques and photos of himself with various dignitaries and celebrities.

From his old office he brought his impressively large desk. It took up a lot of space in his new office. He squeezed in his special little table that he used for his coffeepot, but his five-drawer lateral file cabinet had to go in the garage. Clearing off family doodads and pictures, he placed his reference books on a bookshelf in the family room. He didn't need a printer because he hooked into the printer his son had left in his room. Happily Jack was ready to go.

His plan had been to file only at the end of the day but he found he needed to access the file cabinet that was in the garage more than he had anticipated. It was a hassle to have to go through the house into the garage, deactivating and activating the alarm system each time. At first, he thought the trip would not be a big deal but he found that the frequent treks became a huge frustration. At the end of the day, when he was tired, he often neglected that final trip to the garage to file the day's papers.

He got tired of going to the family room for books. To cut down on trips, Jack started keeping his books on one end of his desk and piling the files on which he was working on the other end.

The trip to his son's printer was annoying as well, so within the first two weeks he bought a printer of his own, thinking that would solve the bulk of the problem. He put it on the coffeepot table and moved the coffeepot into the kitchen.

As he worked in his office, he realized increasingly that he needed a file cabinet and a bookcase in his office. When his wife suggested he get a smaller desk, Jack was offended. His big desk symbolized his significance as an attorney. So he tried moving it to another spot in the room to make more floor space for the other furniture. He tried various configurations but nothing worked.

In the end, the inevitable happened: a trip to the office furniture store for a smaller desk, matching bookcase, and a two-drawer file cabinet. These purchases solved his problem and looked attractive, to boot.

Like many, Jack had failed to appreciate how carefully he had to plan his furniture for his small home office. Also he didn't realize, until he began working, how important it was to have everything conveniently placed for maximum productivity.

Get Rid of Clutter

Many people feel clutter is their biggest hindrance to productivity. They can't move forward until something is done about the papers and other items that hinder them from finding things and accomplishing their goals. Eventually the disarray keeps them from making the kind of money they want to make. In addition, they feel embarrassed in front of co-workers and clients because of the mess. In short, messes become a serious interference.

Many home offices, especially those that are for personal use, end up being more than an office. They can turn into multipurpose rooms, used for guest room furniture, extra storage, children's toys, craft supplies, and the like.

In the office, make sure surfaces such as your desk, credenza, and chairs are clear before you leave for the day. Return files to their appropriate location. Make your office look the way you want it to look when you walk in the next morning.

Save time by storing nonpaper items in the place where you will look for them so nothing is unfindable when you need it. Use the last five minutes before you leave for the day to tidy up.

Offices at business locations are not immune from clutter either.

The "Tooth" about Dr. Franklin's Office

Dr. Franklin had been inundated with samples for her dental clients. She belonged to many associations and was on the mailing lists of myriad manufacturers. She kept tooth-whitening kits, toothpaste, mouthwash, and fluoride capsules to share with her patients. She had booklets about dental health for distribution. In addition, she had models of the mouth and teeth to illustrate procedures to her patients. All the samples, booklets, and models were jumbled together in piles in her patient consultation room.

Dr. Franklin shared a practice with another dentist. She envied him when she saw him sitting grandly behind his desk conferring with a patient in his pristine consultation office, while she was forced to confer in the treatment rooms. In addition to speaking to patients, she would like to use her patient consultation office for educational purposes, showing videos about procedures, but that was impossible. She kept the door closed so no one could see the embarrassing mess.

Cleaning up her consultation office was not only a matter of personal pride but it was a matter of economics as well. If she could confer with patients in the consultation office, her staff could use that time to prepare the treatment room for the next patient. She judged that she would save enough time after each patient to see an additional patient per day. Over a year's time, that would add up to a lot of money.

The problem was not complex but it took a new receptionist's skill and interest to point out the solution. Moving the booklets and samples into clear plastic boxes to the storage room made them easily accessible to the staff to pass out to patients as they exited. She had three shelves added in the consultation room for models and she hung posters on the walls. A computer in the consultation room was available when DVDs or other visuals were appropriate for patient education.

The chief changes were Dr. Franklin's dedication to keep the surfaces in her office clear and her instructions to the staff about how to store and distribute samples and educational materials.

When Dr. Franklin had initially set up her office, she had designed a good plan for the use of space. But she had failed to focus on making it work. Slowly clutter drifted in and the usefulness of the room drifted out. When she refocused and rededicated herself to maintaining the space as she had originally envisioned it, she was able to see more patients as well as give those she saw the proper attention and education.

Taking the time to declutter pays off in future productivity. This is especially true of decluttering papers. That will be dealt with in the following chapter.

Your Turn

Offices exist to help you accomplish your goals. Anything that stands in the way of that happening is a problem that needs to be fixed.

☐ Do you need to get rid of any equipment or furniture in your office? Is there furniture or equipment you need to add to make your office more productive?

☐ Do you need to reorganize the supplies or other items for more efficiency?

☐ If an organized person looked at your office, would he or she feel comfortable? If not, what could you do to meet the expectations of an organized person?

Tips

1. Save time by arranging your furniture and files so that the items you use most often are close to your work station.
2. Use stacking trays to sort papers and periodicals.
3. Keep surfaces clear by storing your office tools in a drawer in your desk.
4. Draw a diagram of the workflow in your office. Arrange your furniture and equipment to follow the diagram.
5. Select comfortable office furniture, ergonomically designed chairs, and glare-free computer screens.

True or false?

1. I have papers on a lot of surfaces.
2. I hesitate to put papers in a filing cabinet for fear I won't be able to find them.
3. I keep my papers in piles so I know where they are at a glance.

If you answered true, true, true to the statements above, say yes to the plans presented in the next chapter.

---

23 organize your papers

*the joy of clear surfaces
and neat files*

Our two greatest problems are gravity and paperwork. We can lick gravity, but sometimes the paperwork is overwhelming.

Dr. Wernher von Braun

There are three reasons to get control of your papers.

1. Organized papers look better than having them strewn around.
2. Having your papers organized frees you from the panic and stress that come when you need an important paper and have little idea where it is.
3. Having papers under control saves you a huge amount of time. The example is often used that if you spend ten minutes a day looking for various papers, by the end of a year, you will have wasted sixty hours—two and a half days, or nearly eight 8-hour working days!

Envisioning Perfection

Look at the piles of paper in your office and ask yourself a question that is similar to what we talked about in chapter 4: *How would my office look if it were perfect?* Envision clear surfaces. Imagine your desk totally free of paper. Do the same with the floor, chairs, file top, credenza, or wherever the papers are stacked. You need to have a visual goal for where you are going.

Before beginning to organize your papers, prioritize the surfaces to be cleared according to:

Organized people are too lazy to look for things. Let's get to be this kind of lazy. Some people call it smart.

which one bothers you most

or

which one would make you feel best if it were cleared up

Select the first surface you are going to deal with. Clear the papers from that surface. Make a rule to yourself that once a surface is clear, you won't put anything back on it until every paper pile in your office has been handled.

As you approach the first area you have chosen, keep in mind that there are only three things you can do with a piece of paper:

1. Throw it away.
2. Act on it—"act" is a verb and requires you to do something.
3. Put it in a file for future reference—"file" is a noun, and each piece of paper will be placed in a labeled file.

What You Will Need

To handle your papers you need some basic supplies:

file cabinet (get the best you can afford so the drawers glide all the way out easily and there is a bar for hanging file folders)

hanging file folders

plastic tabs

Post-it notes

three-ring binder—information journal to hold random information

trash bag

felt-tipped pen

Proceed without Caution

Begin by picking up the first paper from the first pile. If the paper requires action, write on a tab what you need to do, using a verb to indicate what action you will take like "Call Aunt Mary" or "Cancel this subscription." Put the tab on a hanging file folder and place the paper in that folder. It's better to have a folder with one piece of paper in it than to have one folder with lots of papers. All of the action files go in the front of your file drawer. Reference folders follow.

When you first start, you will have a lot of folders, but they will dwindle as you take action. Since you can see each tab easily, you will be inclined to take care of that action.

The rule for your "to-do pile" is that you read every tab, every day. This way nothing slips through the cracks and you don't forget to do an action that may get lost and buried otherwise.

Each action item that is connected with a piece of paper should have its own folder to house the paper, until that action is complete. When you are done with a folder, the plastic tab is popped off and the folder can be reused. Try this. You will love it. It really works!

If the paper in your hand should be filed for reference, make a file tab, label it with a noun like "Gardening" or "Jones

Account" and place it in the file drawer behind the action file folders. Reference will be the largest section.

If the paper is important but truly does not seem to have a category or is not appropriate to file, put the information into a three-ring binder to use as an information journal. Punch three holes in the original piece of paper and put it in the binder in the order in which it appears. Do not try to organize this binder; simply put new items in the front. When you are looking for random information, such as an html code or something needed rarely, it will be in the binder. You will find that the old items in the back may become obsolete as you add new items in the front. You can delete obsolete papers and keep your binder fresh.

If you decide to throw away the paper, put it in the trash bag. If you wish, make a pile beside the shredder to shred later or shred as you go.

These steps form the backbone of successfully handling papers. Remember the four categories for all paper:

Action. Label with a verb and put it in the action file section.

Reference. Label with a noun and put it in the reference section of the file drawer.

Info Journal. Pop into your information journal.

Useless. Toss it!

Rhoda, the Flower Shop Lady

Where your papers are stored makes a huge difference in how efficiently you use your time while you are in your office. At first, keeping papers in piles seems efficient. *Just for now I will put it here*, we think. We don't want to take the time to file it because we think we will remember where it is and be able to get to it easier if it is in a pile within reach. Besides, having it near us on the desk acts as a visual prompt. If it were in a file folder, it might be forgotten. To a limited degree, this starts out working okay. However, when the piles become numerous and tall, the system breaks down, and we find ourselves working off the top of the piles where the papers are fresher and forgetting about the papers that are on the bottom of the pile.

Rhoda was a creative and active owner of a flower shop. Because she was often on the phone taking orders, she had little time to file the papers that came in the mail or were generated each day through her work. She knew she didn't need to keep many of the flyers that came in the mail but she did want to keep a few. So when materials came in, she set them aside to consider later. She also had a pile for customer bills that had been paid, orders that had been filled, and telephone messages.

When the Pile System Fails

Rhoda wouldn't let anybody handle her papers. Her daughter had come home from college and as a surprise had organized them into folders. Rhoda was very upset by the change. Now she couldn't find anything.

In truth, Rhoda had a good system up to a point. Often she would say, "It's about a third of the way down in that pile on the chair." Problems arose when she couldn't find a paper. If she forgot where it was in a pile, there was no handle for locating it. She was in serious trouble.

Rhoda's problem was that the pile system did not work well enough to meet her needs, but she had been afraid to file her papers. Now she was too overwhelmed to know where to begin.

Things Change

When customers came into her shop, Rhoda was embarrassed about how her office and showroom looked. Desperation drove her to change, so rallying her daughter back into the project with stern warnings not to do anything she didn't tell her to do, Rhoda began sorting the papers into two groups: action and reference. Her daughter's job was to write the verbs on the action file labels and the nouns on the reference file labels, as her mother decided the fate of each paper. She slipped the labels into the clear plastic tabs and snapped them onto the holder slots of the hanging file. One pile after another disappeared as the papers took their places in the file folder and then were put into the filing cabinet drawer.

When her daughter commented that it seemed strange to put only one or two papers into a file folder, Rhoda corrected her: "Better that I should be able to find the paper than I should save money on file folders." With this system there was no need for internal manila folders.

Intuitively, Rhoda's daughter began to group the reference hanging file folders into groups—"Vendors," "Clients," "Marketing," and the like. Then she alphabetized those that were in each grouping. Using that system worked well and Rhoda could often locate what she wanted without much trouble just by opening the file drawer. But just to make sure she could find what she needed when she needed it, she had a brilliant idea.

While Rhoda sat at the computer and typed, her daughter called out the names of the file folders one by one in the order they were placed. Now all Rhoda had to do to locate a needed paper was to open the computerized master list of file folders, type in the key word, and tell the computer to search (or find) that paper.

Many papers, and I mean many, went into the circular file (trash can). In each case Rhoda had delayed making a quick decision about them and just hung onto them. Her daughter carried out bag after bag of trash as they were filled.

Cleaning up the paper piles took a lot of time and stamina. It took a lot of hanging file folders and file drawer space. But to Rhoda it was worth it to see her desk, chairs, top of the file cabinet, and floor emerge from under the paper glut.

Rhoda was surprised that being able to see the clear surfaces she had created gave her so much pleasure. Better yet, with her master list she was able to find the papers she needed without fail, and in her action files she could easily read the tabs. Now she could welcome her customers into her shop, even her office, with pride.

Emergency Measures (and Who Doesn't Have Emergencies?)

There's never time to put it away, but there is always time to look for it.

A lot of us have paper emergencies of various kinds that put us in a time crunch. It may be filing our income tax or upcoming audit, an important client, or overdue bills. Sometimes we just get to the end of our paper management rope and feel we have got to get control right away. Our papers need critical care.

Fernando had a special reason for his emergency. When he returned to his home after a long hospital stay, he found six grocery bags full of mail. Most of it was solicitations and useless flyers for sales that had long since passed. But among the junk were important bills now overdue, insurance forms relating to his illness, and an IRS letter.

Even though Fernando was not yet himself physically, the mail couldn't wait. Emergency efforts were called for. He decided to make three piles and he called them yes, no, and maybe.

As he eyeballed his mail without opening the envelopes, he put the papers he needed to address soon into the yes pile. Some were urgent and some were not but he would deal with that later. The pile he labeled maybe were things he wasn't sure about until he opened the envelopes. He put the no pile in a trash bag. In about an hour he had finished the quick sort.

Now he could see the shape of the monster he faced. He went back into his yes pile and pulled out the ones he thought were urgent and handled them as quickly as possible. When that job was finished, he turned his attention to less urgent mail. Then he dealt with the maybe pile, giving it a quick run-through to make sure nothing important was there.

Anytime you are overwhelmed with papers, you can use this stopgap measure of yes, no, and maybe to get a handle on the chaos before you. It does wonders to clarify your thinking and whittle down your paper pile.

Double Trouble with Two Offices

Not all paper problems require a complex system of control. When you take time to examine the problems and design solutions, you may find that your paper problem does not require a complicated solution. Graham was lucky he had somebody who helped him clarify what he needed.

It was another rush day for Graham. A lot of his problem was that he alternated between his home office and his business office. He brought things home to work on during the evening. Sometimes he took his work into the family room, watching TV as he worked. When he left the next day, he frequently had trouble locating the work he had done the night before.

It went the other way as well. Often, when he needed to take work home, he had to scramble to locate the papers he needed in the piles that were around the office. It was not unusual for him to get behind in his daily schedule.

The joke among his clients was that, since Graham was always a half hour late to any appointment, they made it a half hour earlier than they wanted. Because he was dynamic and creative (and had a great product) and his clients enjoyed his jovial personality, mostly they overlooked his problem. Internally Graham felt a personal sense of shame but outwardly he laughed along with the clients as he wrote up their many orders.

His angel of organizing mercy appeared in the form of his visiting college-aged niece, who happened to be named Angela, appropriately enough. Organized by nature, she quickly saw the problems he struggled with and then envisioned and put into practice a simple solution.

She bought file folders in three different colors that were carried in a document carrier. Red was for clients. Yellow was for any paperwork, such as reports, newsletters, trainee evaluations, and other non-client-related material. Green was for anything that had to do with money.

It was not an actual filing system. It was a stopgap emergency measure but it was all Graham needed and it worked wonders. It helped him focus, and he found that it saved him hours of time and mounds of frustration. He kept people waiting less and sometimes he was even on time.

The principles of paper management (color coding, sorting, labeling, storing adequately, and the like) are standard. However, the applications vary depending on your special needs. Taking control of papers in today's world is one of the pillars of organizational success.

Although the computer offers an opportunity to go paperless that many happily embrace, there is a segment of the population that still feel more comfortable with the hard copy, paper approach. For them, when a document slips into the computer desktop, they feel as though it is disappearing. So paper management remains an important concern.

Organization success will bring many good things into your life, among them the opportunity to fulfill your best potential, achieve your goals, take advantage of your opportunities, and fulfill the purposes for which you were created. The next chapter brings into focus the reasons we strive for order in our hurried lives.

Your Turn

☐ Thinking about how your office looks now, write three statements about how your office would look if it were perfect.

☐ Do you need to buy more or better equipment (especially, filing cabinets and hanging files) for your office?

☐ Can you think of a solution for your specific problems? Would it help to ask for somebody else's opinion or suggestion?

Tips

1. Be in-basket wise. Make a definite plan for how you are going to handle the papers in the in-basket.
2. Save important documents only and throw the rest away.
3. Keep files you need to act on in the drawer closest to you or in a hanging file nearby.
4. Make a master list for your file folders.
5. Store your master list as the first folder in the first drawer.
6. When you know a throwaway date, note it at the top of the file before you put it away.
7. Be sure you have all of the supplies you need before you begin to file.

24 make the most of life

manage your opportunities

To be what we are, and to become what we are capable of becoming is the only end of life.

Robert Louis Stevenson

Opportunities come to us all, often unexpectedly. Using tides as a metaphor for opportunities, Shakespeare put it well when he wrote:

There is a tide in the affairs of men
Which, taken at the flood, leads on to fortune;
Omitted, all the voyage of their life
Is bound in shallows and in miseries.

From *Julius Caesar*

This book is written to help those who read it to avoid being stuck in the shallows of life and to allow the flood tides to carry them successfully out into the wide ocean of life.

Opportunity Management

To a certain extent, time management is opportunity management. Most people paddle through life making average progress without disciplining themselves to manage their time. They never realize that if they had been organized, their lives would have been qualitatively different.

Look around in your own experience and you will recall an uncle or someone who somehow "made it" when his siblings did not. You will hear stories of men and women whose lives you admire who have made significant contributions while their classmates did not. Many unknown and unrecognized people have lived lives of quiet significance because they have achieved important lifetime goals for themselves, their families, and for the greater good, while others did not.

"Lucky" Success?

"Luck" (another name for being prepared for unexpected opportunities) sometimes plays a part in success. Natural ability surely helps, and some people have more resources than others. But these are not the axes on which success turns.

More often than not, the power of success lies in mastering the issues dealt with in this book, such as

- goals
- priorities
- discipline
- planning
- preparation

Had successful people not incorporated these organizational basics into their lives, all of the "luck," natural ability, and resources would have been of little use.

When the tide of opportunity came, they were ready. They sailed over the sandbar and entered the ocean while others hesitated, resigning themselves to life in the shallows. If we wish to reach our greatest potential, we cannot afford to ignore the tools of time management that will enable us to take the tides before us.

The research team of Tom Gilovich and Vicki Medvec did a study on what people regret. They found that in the short term, people regret actions that they have done more than inaction on their part. However, as time went by, when people looked back over their lives as a whole, what they regretted most was the things they did not do (omission) rather than what they did do (commission) by a factor of 84 percent to 16 percent. Perhaps this is why the words of John Greenleaf Whittier still resonate after 150 years: "Of all sad words of tongue or pen, the saddest are these: 'It might have been!'"

> By the yard, it's very hard. But inch by inch, it's a cinch.

There is a wonder and wildness to life, and you want to be ready to take full advantage of all that comes your way by managing your life and time wisely. You have only one life to live. Live it with as much dignity, gusto, power, and purpose as possible.

Actually Move Out

Organizing the office, handling interruptions, using a to-do list, managing projects, scheduling wisely, avoiding perfectionism, delegating, and the other areas with which this book has dealt may seem dry and mundane. But as part of the larger picture, they are essential and when you master them, they will yield great value. They are the oil that moves a productive life forward successfully. To use another metaphor, they are the framework on which important goals are structured.

As we said at the beginning of the book, pick out one or two principles and begin working on them. Whether your need for time management centers around your home or your business or both, weave each principle into your life and then come back to this book and move to the next one. Like a butterfly from a cocoon, you will find your higher life slowly but surely begin to emerge.

Revisit the ten principles on a regular basis. Write notes beside each one as a reminder of its application to your life.

1. Dream big
2. Focus: keep the main thing the main thing
3. Do it now
4. Take control of your projects
5. Delegate, delegate, delegate
6. Manage interruptions, distractions, and time wasters
7. Make and use an effective schedule
8. Use the right tools
9. Hang on to a few powerful habits
10. Organize your space

Nothing beats the sense of personal satisfaction that grows as our topsy-turvy life begins to right itself and we align our activities with our real goals and desires.

Looking Higher

Relating to the subject of goal setting, Henry David Thoreau reminds us: "It's not enough to be busy. The question is: What are we busy about?"

Every human being wants to have a significant part in a significant enterprise. People hunger to live purposefully. Time management is an outworking of that yearning.

For the Christian believer, John Piper states clearly, "We waste our lives when we do not weave God into our eating and drinking and every other part by enjoying and displaying him." The "every other part" would include all aspects of our life, such as commuting, filing, working at home or the office, sleeping, and vacationing. When daily activities are seen in this light, they take on a special significance and what we call "time management" becomes life management, opportunity management, for a higher purpose.

Each person must decide the raison d'être of his or her own life. Then each person must bring his or her activities into line with that vision. When this is done, time management becomes more than planners, calendars, and schedules. Time management, with all it involves, becomes a road to significance.

Your Turn

While the iron is hot and your head is full of considerations about how you spend your time, write your mission statement, a few sentences that spotlight your reasons for wanting to maximize your use of time. What motivates you in this great opportunity of living?

What you write does not have to be poetic, all encompassing, or profound. You can always modify or change it later if you wish. Make it a screen saver. Or just jot your thoughts on a card and post it in a prominent place or carry it with you, maybe close to your heart.

Then give yourself a big whoopie! Because just by writing the things you did, you have already begun to make progress toward those goals.

invite others into the story

- Write a review of this book on Amazon.com or some other online book store.
- Buy copies for friends and/or fellow workers for gifts.
- Lead a group using the ten quick lessons in the back of the book.
- Discuss the book in a blog.
- Mention the book in your organizational newsletter.
- Talk the book up or write about it in homeschool circles.
- Put copies in your company's reception area and lounge.
- Think of your own creative ideas and let us know how they work out.

activities for ten time management choices

No matter what is holding you back in your efforts at time management, you can overcome it. Choose to incorporate these ten habits into your life. Your productivity will soar. Your personal satisfaction will soar as well. There is a wonderfully upgraded life waiting for you. Just begin one step at a time to move in that direction. After successfully adding one of the time management choices to your life, go on to the next one.

The ten sessions that follow can be used by groups or individuals. Use them for business groups, club groups, church small groups, or just a bunch of friends who want to improve the quality of their lives. Do one session each time you meet or adjust the sessions to be used in any time frame.

If you have a group, you will need a facilitator to move the group from one activity to another. When sharing, a large group will need to be broken into smaller groups or one-on-one partnerships for the sake of time. The assumption is that those attending will have read the chapters suggested for each lesson, though that is not absolutely necessary. Keep the meetings moving and no longer than necessary to cover the material.

Some of these activities will repeat some of the suggestions at the end of the chapters.

Session 1

dream big

Read chapter 4.
Leader: have a 3×5 card for each member of the group.

Dare to wonder what your life would be like if your time worked out just right, if it were (gasp!) perfect. Don't skip over this as a superfluous exercise. Remember the old saying: He who aims at nothing is likely to hit it. The opposite is also true: He who aims carefully at something is likely to hit it, or at least come very near.

Activity 1—Discuss with your group or consider on your own which if any of the stories in the chapter sounded like you. Divide into groups of two or three to describe your time management concerns. Write two or three sentences spotlighting your chief issues.

_____

_____

_____

Activity 2—What would be your ideal life if your time management were perfect? Ignore any present hindrances. We are dreaming, remember? Tell your partners and then write your dream briefly.

_____

_____

_____

Activity 3—On a 3×5 card, list three specific goals (dreams) and put a target date by each one. The date is not written in stone. Just guess at a date when you would like to finish. Share your goals in your group. Post the card in a conspicuous place at home or work or add what you wrote to your computer desktop. Refer to it often.

Activity 4—At this point, what do you consider your main goal in life? You may call it your sense of purpose or your personal mission statement. As you read further, you may want to refine or modify the purpose you have written here.

_____

_____

_____

focus

keep the main thing the main thing

Read chapter 5.
Leader: have blank paper available.

Creative and interesting people have many areas about which they are enthusiastic. They overextend themselves in their passion for life. Keep the passion but learn how to prioritize so you will accomplish the goals that are most important to you.

Chapter 4 dealt with broad areas of purpose in our lives. On a day-to-day level, however, our goals are more defined by activities we choose to do. If we are not careful, the large overarching purposes in our lives can become blurred by everyday demands. Here is where we bite the bullet and make important choices.

Most of us are not as clueless as George about the fact that there is not enough time to accomplish every single thing we want to do. But each of us has a little George in us. We need to weed out the good and cultivate the best, that for which we have passion.

Activity 1—Choose one of the four methods given in chapter 5—Tournament Format, Priority Quadrants, Prioritize-Your-To-Do-List Approach, Streamlined To-Do-List Approach. Use the method you choose to prioritize your activities, writing them on a sheet of paper. If you are with a group, join those in the group who have chosen the same method as you so you can ask for clarification if you run into questions as you work.

Activity 2—List your top three to five priorities.

_____

_____

_____

Activity 3—Share your findings with one or two people in the group. Tell three or four of the highest priorities and the lowest. If you can see the relationship, explain how your highest priorities fit in with your overall life goal(s) from session 1. Overall life goals may vary little over a lifetime, while priorities tend to vary with the ebb and flow of circumstances.

Conclusion—You have identified the top 20 percent or so of the important things in your life. Make these the focus in your daily decisions concerning how you will spend your time.

Session 3

do it now

Read chapter 9.
Leader: have paper available.

There are two kinds of procrastination that plague us all: procrastination of the urgent and less critical but chronic procrastination. No matter what kind is holding you back from doing what needs to be done when it needs to be done, you can get yourself unstuck.

Activity 1—Most of us procrastinate from time to time. Which of the four roots of procrastination, given in the first part of chapter 9, seem to fit your behavior? Are there any other factors that are part of procrastination on your part?

_____

_____

_____

Activity 2—Read over the twelve reasons given for procrastinating, starting with "Dull and Boring." Choose one or more that are similar to what has been part of your recent experience and note the suggestions for overcoming your issue. On the lines below, briefly identify the projects you have been putting off. Continue the list on another sheet of paper if there are more than three. Add briefly what techniques you will try and when you plan to have the job completed. Share your decisions with someone in the group or an interested friend.

Needs to Be Done	How and When I Will Get It Done
1. _____	1. _____
2. _____	2. _____
3. _____	3. _____

Activity 3—Look over the quickie tips for overcoming procrastination. Identify several that you think will work for you on a regular basis. Tell a partner or friend which ones they are. Jot them down as a reminder.

_____

_____

_____

take control
of your projects

Read chapters 10, 11, and 12.
Leader: This session requires material for completion. For activity 2, a three-ring binder and paper will be needed or access to a computer. Print out copies of the Project Master List form and the Project Sheet from the website.

Some projects are simple and it is easy to let the ball drop on these. Some projects are complicated and we need a method to clarify the steps. You will be surprised at how your life will move forward as you apply the principles found in these chapters to all of your projects.

Do you have a project that you are having difficulty starting or completing? You may have to think a while before you come up with one because the uncompleted project has been hanging on so long you have pushed it way to the back of your mind. You may have almost given up on the idea of doing it. Look back at session 3 if you need to be reminded of a project you need to finish.

After you have chosen a project, write down the final outcome you want for the project.

Activity 1—Mind Mapping

Mind mapping will help you break through the confusion about a project that has held you back. On a piece of paper, use the mind mapping technique, described in chapter 10, to think through your project. Don't worry about the details of this technique. Adapt the concept to meet your needs and move forward.

If this works well for you, you may wish to continue by turning it into a time line, writing an outline, or putting the steps in your planner.

Activity 2—Project Notebook

For a paper notebook, you will need a three-ring binder and paper. Or you may decide to use a computer folder instead.

- Prepare a project notebook (or computer folder).
- Fill in the Project Master List form; then fill in the Project Sheet—both forms are found in chapter 11. You may use the forms as they are or modify them to meet your needs.

Activity 3—To-Do List

Draw by hand or create by computer a to-do list, as described in chapter 12. Decide on headings for the quadrants that fit your lifestyle schedule. Find a place to keep your list for easy access and begin using it.

Session 5

delegate, delegate, delegate

Read chapter 13.

Should you delegate a responsibility? To whom? How do you go about it? Delegating well so you can use your time efficiently is an important part of a life well lived. The key? Just do it!

Activity 1—List several activities that are a part of your personal or business life at this time, which you can delegate or partially delegate.

1. _____

2. _____

3. _____

4. _____

5. _____

Activity 2—Note the five areas mentioned on page 136 where Roy could have improved his delegation to Clement.

1. Set a clear objective.
2. Give clear instructions.
3. Set deadlines and checkpoints.
4. Clarify responsibility and authority.
5. Give feedback; follow up.

Describe a situation in your life where you can delegate to your advantage. Describe in writing, as well as telling another person, how you can do each step. If you are part of a group, each person should choose a personal situation.

1. _____
2. _____
3. _____
4. _____
5. _____

manage interruptions, distractions, and time wasters

Read chapters 14 and 15.

None of us lives on a desert island. In this era of electronic communication, we are more likely to be interrupted than ever before. In addition, internal distractions creep in to dissipate our time. These are often overlooked because they are incidental parts of our day. Focus in on the interruptions you experience and how they can be handled.

Activity 1—Make a list of the kinds of distractions/interruptions/time wasters you experience on a daily basis. Put an * by the one or ones that are the biggest problem.

Problem (Activity 1)	Possible Solution (Activity 2)
_____	_____
_____	_____
_____	_____
_____	_____
_____	_____
_____	_____
_____	_____

If you are doing this as a group, set a timer and allow the participants one minute to make the list. Share your list with the group.

Activity 2—Take each interruption type (for example, phone call, meetings, email), and come up with a possible solution for each one. Write the solutions above. In a group, allow 3–5 minutes for this activity. Share your solutions with a small group or one-on-one.

Activity 3—As you consider solutions, write your favorite(s). Often there are several. Begin to implement them in your daily life.

To avoid _____, I will _____
_____.

To avoid _____, I will _____
_____.

To avoid _____, I will _____
_____.

Session 7

make and use
an effective schedule

Read chapters 16 and 17.
Leader: a daily planner is needed for this session.

A well-crafted schedule is a wonderful thing. It's like a powerful engine in a car and will move your life forward.

Activity 1—Make a list of the main things you have to do during a typical week. Divide your list into those activities that are personal and those that are work related.

Personal	Work
_____	_____
_____	_____
_____	_____
_____	_____
_____	_____

Personal	Work
_____	_____
_____	_____
_____	_____
_____	_____

Activity 2—Next to each item listed, write whether it's a fixed commitment or a flexible commitment. (Show your list to a member of the group.)

Activity 3—Take out your planner. First, write in all of the fixed activities for the upcoming week. Next, write in all of the flexible activities, assigning each one a specific time to accomplish.

Make it a point to use your planner in this way on a regular basis.

Try using this approach for a week. Make adjustments where necessary. Share your results with the group.

Session 8

use the right tools

Read chapter 18.

To have the greatest success in sticking to a schedule, you need the right tools. Whether you develop them yourself or buy what is on the market, the right tools will be invaluable. Some people don't want to be bothered with tools. Bad idea. Check out what is available and choose what meets your need and your personality.

Activity 1—Make a list of all of the tools you think are needed to run your office. Divide the list into two columns. Column 1: Tools I already have / Column 2: Tools I need to purchase.

Tools I Have	Tools I Need
_____	_____
_____	_____
_____	_____

Tools I Have	Tools I Need
_____	_____
_____	_____
_____	_____
_____	_____
_____	_____
_____	_____

Activity 2—Make a list of the duplicate or unnecessary tools you have in your office and elsewhere in your home. Call a charity or take them to a charity collection center.

If you are in a group, let each person make a list of the items they want to discard on a piece of paper. Pass the paper around. Have others in the group write their names down next to any item they want or need.

Retrieve your paper. Bring that item for them the next session. The benefit is that you will get rid of an extra (clutter) item, and your fellow participant can get a needed item. Now that's going green!

hang on to a few powerful habits

Read chapter 20.

People who manage their time well have developed a few consistently applied and useful habits. Weaving some of what you learn in this chapter into your life will free you from unnecessary time wasters.

Activity 1—Write one thing you want to gain and one pain you want to avoid by improving your use of time. If you are with a group, give the details of what you want to gain and avoid.

Gain to achieve: _____

Pain to avoid: _____

Activity 2—Name several habits at home or office that are part of your regular routine and that you find beneficial. Write them below and share them if you are with a group.

_____

_____

_____

Activity 3—What is your reaction to the three powerful habits the authors recommend in this chapter—the thirty-second rule, putting something back quickly when you get it out, and keeping surfaces clear? Could you adopt these habits? State specifically how you are going to apply them to your life.

_____

_____

_____

Session 10

organize your space

Read chapters 21, 22, and 23.

"Stuff" in the way, "stuff" to be cared for—these impede and demand our time. Whether papers are piling up in your office or out-of-place items are messing up your home, decluttering your life will free you to do what is really important.

Activity 1—Visualize your office or another room in your home. Now imagine what it would look like if it were "perfect." Write this vision down. If you are in a group, share this with someone.

_____

_____

_____

Activity 2—Now think about the surfaces in the same room. List every single surface in the room (example: floor, shelves, chairs, counters, credenza top, and so on). Visualize what each surface would look like if it were clear of clutter.

Priority   Surface

_____   _____

_____   _____

_____   _____

_____   _____

_____   _____

_____   _____

_____   _____

_____   _____

Activity 3—Prioritize the surfaces to clear, starting with the most important. To the left, number each of the surfaces in the list above in the order in which you will declutter them. Make a commitment to yourself or to someone else that you will clear the surfaces in order until done.

resources

Allen, David. *Getting Things Done*, 2003.

Barnes, Emilie. *The 15-Minute Organizer*, 1991.

Covey, Stephen R. *The 7 Habits of Highly Effective People*, 2004.

Covey, Stephen R., and A. Roger Merrill. *First Things First*, 1999.

Culp, Stephanie. *How to Get Organized When You Don't Have the Time*, 1986.

Davidson, Jeff. *The Complete Idiot's Guide to Managing Your Time*. 3rd ed., 2001.

Dodd, Pamela, and Doug Sundheim, *The 25 Best Time-Management Tools and Techniques*, 2005.

Douglass, Merrill, and Donna Douglass. *Manage Your Time, Your Work, Yourself*, 1993.

Eisenberg, Ronni. *Organize Yourself*, 1986.

Johnson, Spencer. *One Minute for Yourself*, 1998.

Lakein, Alan. *How to Control Your Time and Your Life*, 1973.

Lockwood, Georgene. *The Complete Idiot's Guide to Organizing Your Life*. 4th ed., 2005.

Mackenzie, Alec. *The Time Trap*, 1997.

Mancini, Marc. *Time Management: 24 Techniques to Make Each Minute Count at Work*, 2007.

Mayer, Jeffrey. *If You Haven't Got the Time to Do It Right, When Will You Find the Time to Do It Over?* 1990.

_____. *Winning the Fight between You and Your Desk*, 1993.

McGee-Cooper, Ann. *Time Management for Unmanageable People*, 1993.

Merson, Len. *The Instant Productivity Toolkit*, 2005.

Morgenstern, Julie. *Making Work Work*, 2004.

_____. *Never Check E-Mail in the Morning*, 2005.

_____. *Time Management from the Inside Out*, 2006.

Silber, Lee. *Time Management for the Creative Person*, 1998.

Smallin, Donna. *The One-Minute Organizer Plain and Simple*, 2004.

Smith, Hyrum W. *The 10 Natural Laws of Successful Time and Life Management*, 1994.

Snead, Lynne, and Joyce Wycoff. *To Do, Doing, Done!* 1997.

Starr, Meryl, and Thayer Allyson Gowdy. *The Personal Organizing Workbook*, 2006.

Taylor, Harold. *Making Time Work for You*, 1981.

Tracy, Brian. *Eat That Frog!: 21 Great Ways to Stop Procrastinating and Get More Done*, 2007.

_____. *Goals! How to Get Everything You Want*, 2004.

Tullier, Michelle. *The Complete Idiot's Guide to Overcoming Procrastination*, 1999.

Volk, Helen. *De-Clutter, De-Stress Your Life*, 2001.

Walsh, Peter. *It's All Too Much*, 2007.

Winston, Stephanie. *The Organized Executive*, 1994.

Web Sites and Online Articles

http://en.wikipedia.org/wiki/Time_management

http://www.mindtools.com/pages/main/newMN_HTE.htm

http://www.studygs.net/timman.htm

http://www.time-management-guide.com/

http://www.managementhelp.org/prsn_prd/time_mng.htm

http://blog.penelopetrunk.com/2006/12/10/10-tips-for-time-management-in-a-multitasking-world/

http://www.studygs.net/schedule/

Sandra Felton, The Organizer Lady, is a pioneer in the field of organizing. She is the founder of Messies Anonymous and the author of many books including *Organizing Magic*. Sandra lives in Alachua, Florida.

Marsha Sims is a national speaker who has taught seminars on time management and organization, managing the front desk, and projects and priorities. She has been a professional organizer for fifteen years as the founder and president of her Miami-based company, Sort-It-Out, Inc.

Say good-bye to the stress of mess—
for good!

Get rid of compulsive clutter for life!

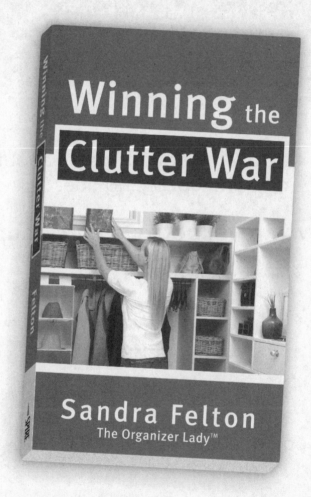